Time to Start

Learn from Your Errors!

より自然な英語習得のための英語演習

樋口　千春

村田　倫子

NAN'UN-DO

Time to Start

Learn from Your Errors!

Chiharu Higuchi / Noriko Murata

©2020 All Rights Reserved

音声ファイル
無料 DL
のご案内

このテキストの音声を無料で視聴（ストリーミング）・ダウンロードできます。自習用音声としてご活用ください。
以下のサイトにアクセスしてテキスト番号で検索してください。

https://nanun-do.com テキスト番号 [**512017**]

※ 無線 LAN（WiFi）に接続してのご利用を推奨いたします。

※ 音声ダウンロードは Zip ファイルでの提供になります。
　お使いの機器によっては別途ソフトウェア（アプリケーション）の導入が必要となります。

Time to Start 音声ダウンロードページは
左記の QR コードからもご利用になれます。

Read by

Emma Howard（英）
Dominic Allen

はじめに

　皆さんの中には，英語を勉強しても一向に上達しない，英語を何度聞いても聞き取れない，といった経験をされた方がいるかもしれません。本書は「初級者によくみられる英語表現の間違い」をテーマに取り上げ，会話文，読解，リスニングなどバラエティに富んだ設問を繰り返し解くことで定着力を高めていくことを目指すテキストになっています。学習者の多くがつまずきやすい「間違い」は母語干渉の影響が大きく，特に初級者では，言語転移・同義語の誤使用が多く見られます。これらを正しく認識することは，英語と日本語の違いを学ぶことにもつながり，それぞれの言語の独自性に興味を持つきっかけになります。このテキストを学習することで，「間違い」に自ら気づき，平易な問題を解き進め「間違い」の原因を理解し，正しく再認識することを最終目標としています。

　ユニットが進むにつれて，基本的な問題の反復練習こそが英語上達の鍵だと気づかれることでしょう。大問 6，7 は皆さんにとって初めての形式かも知れません。まず書かれている英文を日本語に直し，その内容を理解した後にその英文を聞いてもらいます。最初に内容がわかれば意外と聞き取りが楽になりますので，リスニングが苦手な人でも安心して取り組めるよう構成されています。また，各ユニットの最後は TOEIC® L&R Test および TOEIC Bridge® L&R Tests 形式の演習を使用しています。皆さんが将来受験する際の助けとなれば幸いです。

　最後に，本書の企画案にご快諾をいただきました株式会社南雲堂の皆様方，およびご担当の伊藤宏実氏には編集・出版に多大なご尽力を賜りました。この場をお借りして心から感謝の意を表します。

著者

CONTENTS

Unit 1 え！「アルバイト」って英語じゃなかったの？

Q. 以下の日本語を英語にしましょう。（60 秒）

1.	バイト		5.	リュックサック
2.	ドア		6.	ニアピン
3.	ハンドル		7.	ナイター
4.	ストーブ		8.	冬のコート

上の 8 つの問題からわかったことは何ですか？次の（　　　）に適切な日本語を入れましょう。

Target （　　　　　　　　　　　　　　　）は，そのままのスペリングで正しい英単語になるとは限らない。

---

1 次の会話文の中に英語の間違えが 1 つあります。間違えている語（句）に下線を引き，（　　　）に適切な英語を書き入れましょう。

1. Judy: I like Ms. Hirai's geography class. Her lessons are easy to understand.
   平井先生の地理のクラス好きよ。先生の授業はわかりやすいよね。

   Takuya: Yes. She gives us prints at the beginning of every lesson.
   そうだね。先生は毎回授業の始めにプリントを配るよね。（　　　　　　　　）

2. Bob: Did you check your email today?　今日，メールをチェックしましたか？
   Mariko: Yes. I received a claim email from one of our clients.
   はい。顧客の一人からクレームのメールを受け取りました。（　　　　　　　　）

3. Cathy: Here's my favorite photo from my university days. Do you want to see it?
   大学生時代のお気に入りの写真があるんだけれど。見たい？

   Takako: I can't believe this! You were very smart.
   信じられない！あなたすごくスマートだったのね。　　　（　　　　　　　　）

4. Carol: You're working a lot these days, aren't you?　最近よく働いているわね。
   Shinji: Well, I'd like to have my home in the suburbs.
   郊外にマイホームが欲しいのです。　　　　　　　　　（　　　　　　　　）

5. John: I want to eat something sweet.　何か甘いものが食べたいな。
   Mari: Good idea! Let's go and buy a dozen shoe creams.
   いいね！シュークリームを 1 ダース買いに行きましょう。　（　　　　　　　　）

2 語群から適切な語（句）を選び（　　）に書き入れ，日本文に合う英文を完成させましょう。

1

> claims / complaints / cream puffs / handouts / my home
> my own house / prints / shoe creams / slim / smart

1. 私は郊外にマイホームが欲しいです。　　1をきちんとマスターすると2が簡単に解けるよ。

   I would like to have (　　　　　　　　　　　　) in the suburbs.

2. 私はシュークリームが大好きです。

   I love (　　　　　　　　　).

3. 先生は宿題に関するプリントを生徒たちに配りました。

   The teacher gave the class (　　　　　　　　　　) about the homework.

4. 彼は若い頃はスマートだった。

   He was (　　　　　　　　　) when he was young.

5. 今月は製品についてのクレームが5件ありました。

   There were five (　　　　　　　　　) about our products this month.

2

> air conditioner / concents / cooler / hamburger / Hamburg steak
> no make / no sleeve / outlets / sleeveless / without makeup

1. この部屋にはいくつコンセントが設置されていますか？

   How many (　　　　　　　　　) does this room have?

2. 私はノースリーブのドレスが好きです。

   I'd like a (　　　　　　　　) dress.

3. 彼女は日曜日にはいつもノーメイクで散歩します。

   She always takes a walk (　　　　　　　　　　) on Sundays.

4. クーラーをつけてもらえる？

   Can you turn on the (　　　　　　　　　)?

5. 私は夕食にハンバーグを食べました。

   I ate a (　　　　　　　　) for dinner.

3　1 ～ 10 の英語を後半 a ～ j と線でつないで，意味を成す英文を完成させましょう。

1.	John was slim	·	· a	the class handouts.
2.	Mary is wearing	·	· b	in my apartment.
3.	I need more outlets	·	· c	a sleeveless dress.
4.	Satoshi would like to have	·	· d	his own house in Tokyo.
5.	The teacher gave	·	· e	when he was young.

▶▶1 ～ 5 で作った英文を日本語に直しましょう。

1. _____
2. _____
3. _____
4. _____
5. _____

6.	You should make a complaint	·	· f	doesn't work.
7.	The air conditioner	·	· g	without makeup.
8.	Your face is very beautiful	·	· h	my grandmother's Hamburg steak.
9.	I like to eat	·	· i	are very delicious.
10.	The cream puffs	·	· j	about their service.

▶▶6 ～ 10 で作った英文を日本語に直しましょう。

6. _____
7. _____
8. _____
9. _____
10. _____

4 (A)〜(D) の 4 つの短い音声を聴き，写真の内容を最も適切に表現しているものを
1 つ選びましょう。

ノースリーブは英語で何だったかな？

1 (A) (B) (C) (D)   **2** (A) (B) (C) (D)

5 次に読まれる会話文を聴いてその質問に対する応答として最も適切を思われるものを，
(A)〜(D) の 4 つの選択肢の中から 1 つ選びましょう。

1 1. What did the man buy for Mary?

   (A) Shoe polish

   (B) Cream puffs

   (C) Shoe creams

   (D) Whipped cream

  2. Who opened the box?

誰が箱を開けたのか名前を聞き取ろう！

   (A) Mary

   (B) May

   (C) Kenji

   (D) Kenta

2 1. Did the man watch a night game, the Mariners vs. the Dodgers?

   (A) Yes, he did.

   (B) Yes, he does.

   (C) No, he didn't.

   (D) No, he doesn't.

  2. What is a nighter?

会話文を聞き取らなくても解答できる問題だよ！

   (A) It's an English word that means a night person.

   (B) It's an English word that means "a night game."

   (C) It isn't an English word but a Japanese English word.

   (D) It isn't an English word but a baseball word.

6A （　　）に適切な日本語を入れて，英会話文を日本語に直しましょう。

Masaki: I'll have to take biology class again.

Janet: Again?

Masaki: I did cunning and failed the class.

Janet: Cunning? What do you mean?

Masaki: I acted unfairly in the exam to get a good score.

Janet: I see. You should use an English word "cheat." Anyway, let's eat out for a change after class.

Masaki: Well, I have to work part-time at a gasoline stand today. How about tomorrow? I'd like to go to a family restaurant and eat "morning."

Janet: Well, I guess that's a gas station not a gasoline stand. And you want to eat a "breakfast special" not "morning." Would you like anything else?

Masaki: Hamburger, fried poteto and soft cream for dessert.

Janet: Oh, dear, french fries not fried poteto. And soft serve ice cream not soft cream.

Masaki: Oh, they are Japanese English words, aren't they?

雅紀：¹（　　　　　　　　　　　　　　　　　　　　）。

ジャネット：また？

雅紀：カンニングしちゃって単位を落としだんだ。

ジャネット：cunning？どういう意味？

雅紀：いい点数を取りたくて試験中に不正をしちゃったんだ。

ジャネット：なるほど。英語の 'cheat' を使うべきね。とにかく²（

　　　　　　　　　　　　　　　　　　　）。

雅紀：えーと，今日はガソリンスタンドでバイトなんだ。明日はどう？ファミレスに行ってモーニングを食べたいな。

ジャネット：えっと，gasoline stand ではなくて gas station。そして morning ではなく breakfast special。

他に何か食べたいものある？

雅紀：ハンバーガー，フライドポテトそれにデザートにソフトクリーム。

ジャネット：あらあら，fried poteto じゃなくて french fries。soft cream じゃなくて soft serve ice cream よ。

雅紀：ああ，それらは和製英語なんだね。

6B 次に読まれる会話文を聴いてその質問に対する応答として最も適切と思われるものを，(A)〜(D) の 4 つの選択肢の中から 1 つ選びましょう。

 6

1. What did the guy do during the test?
   (A) Failed his English lesson
   (B) Ate french fries
   (C) Did cunning
   (D) Cheated on the exam

2. Where does the guy work part-time?
   (A) At a restaurant
   (B) At a gasoline stand
   (C) At a gas station
   (D) At a pub

   選択肢の和製英語に引っかからないように。

3. What will the guy and the girl probably do tomorrow?
   (A) Go to a party
   (B) Go to a gas station
   (C) Go to a restaurant
   (D) Go to a library

   TOEIC では「次の行動」を尋ねる問題が出題されることが多いよ。
   Ex.1) What will the man probably do next?
   Ex.2) What will the woman most likely do?

~ *Take a Break* ~

 次の英文はアメリカに短期留学している日本人・拓哉とメアリーの会話なのですが，メアリーが怒っているようです。その理由は何でしょうか？

At the party venue（パーティー会場にて）

Mary:　　Hi, Takuya. This is a great party, isn't it? There are many elegantly dressed guests.

Takuya:　Yes. I like your nice bottom.

Mary:　　What!! *Excuse me?

　　　　　　　　　　　　　　　　　　　　*Excuse me?: もう一回言ってくれませんか？

Unit 2　「足の指」は "foot finger" だよね?

Q: 日本語に合うように (　　) に適切な体の部分を表す英単語を書き入れましょう。(60秒)

1.	彼は**首**を横に振って「いいえ」と言った。 He shook his (　　　　) and said "No."
2.	**顔**を窓から出さないようにしてください。 Please don't put your (　　　　) out of the window.
3.	父は5本**指**のソックスが好きだ。 My father likes socks with five (　　　　).
4.	彼女は階段から落ちて**腰**を骨折しました。 She fell downstairs and broke her (　　　　).

上の4つの問題からわかったことは何ですか? 次の (　　) に適切な日本語を入れましょう。

Target 日本語の名詞は (　　　　　　　) 置きかえると, 状況により正しい英語にならない場合がある。

---

1 次の会話文の中に英語の間違えが1つあります。間違えている語に下線を引き, (　　) に適切な英語を書き入れましょう。

1. Aki: The master of this Japanese pub restaurant is so kind.
　　　　ここの居酒屋のマスターはすごく優しいわね。

　John: I think so. I want to come again.　そうだね。また来たいね。
　　　　　　　　　　　　　　　　　　　　　　　(　　　　　　　　　　)

2. Andy: How did the exams go?　試験の出来はどうだった?

　Tomoko: Well, they went well, but I made a single miss in English.
　　　　え～っと, 良くできたけれど, 英語で1問ミスしちゃった。(　　　　　　)

3. John: Excuse me, where is the nearest post office?
　　　　すみません, いちばん近い郵便局はどこにありますか?

　Naoko: It's next to the alcohol shop.　酒屋の隣です。　(　　　　　　)

4. Sam: How is your new part-time job at the convenience store?
　　　　新しいコンビニの仕事はどう?

　Akiko: Well, I'm always busy because there are a lot of visitors.
　　　　うん, 大勢のお客さんが来るからいつも忙しいのよ。　(　　　　　　)

5. Joseph: What did you do during summer vacation?　夏休みに何をしたの?

　Mari: I went back to my country in Kumamoto.　熊本の田舎へ帰ったわよ。
　　　　　　　　　　　　　　　　　　　　　　　(　　　　　　　　　　)

2 語群から適切な語を選び（　　）に書き入れ，日本文に合う英文を完成させましょう。
ただし文頭にくる語も小文字で示してあります。

> bottom / country / customer / hip / hometown /
> manager / master / miss / mistake / visitor / waist

1. **a.** レストランの店長はすごくいい人だ。

   The (　　　　　　　　　　) of the restaurant is very nice.

   b. 野田さんはフェンシングの達人です。

   Mr. Noda is a (　　　　　　　　　　　　) of fencing.

2. **a.** 私は科学で1問ミスしました。

   I made a (　　　　　　　　　　) in science.

   b. 南先生が私たちの英語の先生です。

   (　　　　　　　　　　) Minami is our English teacher.

3. **a.** その年老いた女性は尻もちをつきました。

   The old woman fell on her (　　　　　　　　　　　).

   b. 彼女はバナナの皮で滑って腰を骨折しました。

   She slipped on a banana peel and broke her (　　　　　　　　).

4. **a.** 彼は，このイタリアンレストランの常連客です。

   He is a regular (　　　　　　　　　) at this Italian restaurant.

   b. 先月，カナダからの訪問客がありました。

   I had a (　　　　　　　　　) from Canada last month.

5. **a.** 私は将来田舎に住みたい。

   I want to live in the (　　　　　　　　　) in the future.

   b. 私は仕事を辞めて熊本の田舎に帰りました。

   I quit my job and went back to my (　　　　　　　　　) in Kumamoto.

~ *Take a Break* ~ 答え

拓哉はメアリーのボトム（ズボン）を褒めたつもりだったのですが，bottom は「底」や「お尻」を意味します。
メアリーが怒るのも無理ないですね。

3 1～10の英語を後半a～jと線でつないで，意味を成す英文を完成させましょう。

1. John got   ·   · **a**   always right.

2. The customer is   ·   · **b**   a master's degree.

3. Is Mary the manager   ·   · **c**   with her hands on her hips.

4. I studied for the final exams,   ·   · **d**   of the flower shop?

5. Mary often stands   ·   · **e**   but I made some mistakes.

▶▶ 1～5で作った英文を日本語に直しましょう。

1. _____

2. _____

3. _____

4. _____

5. _____

6. I will see Miss Kato   ·   · **f**   her hometown in Nagano.

7. The museum is   ·   · **g**   in the country in the future.

8. These pants are too big   ·   · **h**   around the waist.

9. Rika went back to   ·   · **i**   for the first time in a while.

10. Tom wants to live   ·   · **j**   full of student visitors.

▶▶ 6～10で作った英文を日本語に直しましょう。

6. _____

7. _____

8. _____

9. _____

10. _____

4 (A)～(D) の 4 つの短い音声を聴き，写真の内容を最も適切に表現しているものを 1 つ選びましょう。

1 (A) (B) (C) (D)　　　**2** (A) (B) (C) (D)

5 次に読まれる会話文を聴いてその質問に対する応答として最も適切と思われるものを，(A)～(D) の 4 つの選択肢の中から 1 つ選びましょう。

1 1. What did the woman do last week?

最初の女性の発話を集中して聞こう。

    (A) She gave finals to her students.

    (B) She got a perfect score on her finals.

    (C) She had a post-exam vacation.

    (D) She had term-end exams.

  2. How many mistakes did the woman make?

    (A) Only one

    (B) Two

    (C) Three

    (D) No mistakes

2 1. What is the man's favorite subject?

    (A) Geology

    (B) Biology

    (C) Science

    (D) Geography

  2. What does Ms. Hirai give at the beginning of every lesson?

    (A) Geography textbooks

    (B) Her favorite books

    (C) Materials for her lesson

    (D) Reference books

6A 図表と英文メールを読み，対応する日本語の（　　）に適切な表現を書き入れましょう。

> ここで取り組むグラフィック（図表）問題は TOEIC で出題されるよ。（図表の種類は，予定表，割引クーポン，グラフなど）まず，何についての図表なのかを理解しよう。

Seattle Event Planning, Co.
Birthday Party

Party package includes party invitations, party games, a music session, a birthday cake, two slices of pizza and french fries.

Package price is $15.00 per child based on a 10-child minimum.

Dear Ms. Green

Hello. I hope you are in good health. I heard your husband moved to Boston two months ago. You and your son still stay in Seattle, right?

It is October once again. Last year you had a birthday party for your son on October 15th. If you would like to have your son's birthday party around the same time this year, please fill out the form and send it to us. If you have any questions, you can give us a call at 555-876-5432.

P.S.: We will not charge you $15.00 for your son this year.

Lisa Hammond
Seattle Event Planning, Co.

シアトルイベント企画社
[1] (　　　　　　　　　)

パーティーパッケージには，招待状，パーティーゲーム，音楽演奏，バースデーケーキ，ピザ 2 切と [2] (　　　　　　　　　) が含まれます。
パッケージ料金は最低 10 人からうけたまわり，お子様お一人につき [3] (　　　　　　) です。

グリーン様

こんにちは。お元気にお過ごしのことと存じます。ご主人が 2 か月前 [4] (　　　　　　) に移られたのですね。奥様と息子さんはまだ [5] (　　　　　　) にいらっしゃるのですよね。

10 月がまたやってまいりました。去年，[6] (　　) 月 [7] (　　) 日に息子さんの誕生日パーティーを開いていただきました。今年も同じ時期に息子さんの誕生会を開かれるつもりであれば [8] (　　　　　　　　　　) いただきお送りください。何かご質問がありましたら 555-876-5432 にお電話ください。

追伸　今年は息子さんの分の [9] (　　　　　　　　　　　　　)。

リサ　ハモンド
シアトルイベント企画社

6B 次に読まれる英文を聴いてその質問に対する応答として最も適切と思われるものを，(A)〜(D) の 4 つの選択肢の中から 1 つ選びましょう。 11

Seattle Event Planning, Co.
Birthday Party

Party package includes party invitations, party games, a music session,
a birthday cake, two slices of pizza and french fries.
Package price is $15.00 per child based on a 10-child minimum.

---

1. Where does Ms. Green live now?
   (A) Seattle
   (B) Santiago
   (C) Bangkok
   (D) Boston

2. When did Ms. Green have their son's birthday party last year?
   (A) October 15th
   (B) October 5th
   (C) November 15th
   (D) November 5th

3. How much will the birthday party cost if Ms. Green invites 20 children?
   (A) $150
   (B) $200
   (C) $300
   (D) $315

聞き取れなかった人は 6A に戻って確認しよう。
1 人でいくらかかるのか書いてあるよ。

 ~ Take a Break ~

英作のワンポイントレッスン

このユニットでは，日本語の名詞と同じ意味を持つ英単語の名詞に置きかえても正しい英語表現にならないケースを取り上げました。これらはすべて，両単語の意味のズレによるものでした。また，名詞を使わない方が自然な英語になる場合も多く存在します。以下は，学習者が間違えやすい例です。

1. 私は昨夜，かなり具合が悪かった。
   I was in a very bad condition last night. → ○ I was sick last night.

2. 朝，シャワーを浴びるのは私の習慣です。
   It is my habit to take a shower in the morning. → ○ I usually take a shower in the morning.

「青リンゴ」は "A blue apple" でいいの?

Q: 日本文に合うように (　) に適切な語を入れましょう。(15 秒)

1.	私は朝食に青リンゴを 1 個食べます。	I eat one (　　　　) apple for breakfast.
2.	私は少し白髪があります。	I have a few (　　　　) hairs.
3.	君は顔色が真っ青だ。	You are as (　　　　) as a sheet.

「信号は青だ」は "The traffic light is green." だよ!

上の英文からわかったことは何ですか?自由に書いてみましょう。

Target (　　　　　　　　　　　　　　　　　　　　　　　　　　　　)

---

1 次の会話文の中に英語の間違えが 1 つあります。間違えている語に下線を引き,(　) に適切な英語を書き入れましょう。

1. Judy: Do you like your job?　仕事は好きですか?

   Takuya: Yes. I like the job, but the pay is very cheap.　ええ。でも給料がすごく安いです。

   (　　　　　　　　　　　　)

2. Bob: John talks to me nicely.　ジョンは私に親切に話しかけてくれます。

   Mariko: He is nice, and his jokes are interesting.　彼はいい人でジョークがおもしろいわ。

   (　　　　　　　　　　　　)

3. Cathy: Do you live alone?　一人暮らしなの?

   Takuo: Yes. I live alone in a narrow room.　そうだよ。狭い部屋で一人暮らしをしているよ。

   (　　　　　　　　　　　　)

4. Carol: Are you going to have a party at your house this weekend?

   週末あなたの家でパーティーするの?

   Shinji: Yes. But my room is dirty. Can you come over and help me clean?

   うん。でも部屋が散らかっているんだ。家に来て掃除を手伝ってくれない?

   (　　　　　　　　　　　　)

5. John: What did you do during the holidays?　休暇には何をしたの?

   Mari: I took a little trip to Taiwan.　台湾に小旅行に行きました。

   (　　　　　　　　　　　　)

2　(　　) から適切な表現を選び○で囲んで，日本文に合う英文を完成させましょう。

1.　その市場調査は興味深いものでした。

The market research (was interested / was interesting).

2.　彼は今日の講義に退屈しました。

He (was bored / was boring) with today's lecture.

3.　研究室での実験はワクワクするものでした。

The *experiment in the *laboratory (was exciting / was excited).

*experiment: 実験　*laboratory: 研究室

4.　私はその発見に驚きました。

I (was surprised / was surprising) at the discovery.

5.　その出来事は大変ショックだったので信じられませんでした。

The event (was too shocking / was too shocked) to believe.

3　1〜5の英語を後半a〜eと線でつないで，意味を成す英文を完成させましょう。

1.　His salary　・	・ a	is high.
2.　Her room　・	・ b	lived in a small room.
3.　A newly married couple　・	・ c	is messy.
4.　The river　・	・ d	is narrow here but is very wide near its mouth.
5.　Her joke　・	・ e	was funny.

▶▶ 1〜5で作った英文を日本語に直しましょう。

1.　_____

2.　_____

3.　_____

4.　_____

5.　_____

4 （　　）に適切な語を書き入れ，日本文に合う英文を完成させましょう。

1. **a.** We were really (　　　　　　　　　　　　　　　) at the baseball game yesterday.
   私たちは昨日の野球の試合で本当にわくわくしました。

   b. Yesterday's Yokohama-Hanshin game was very (　　　　　　　　　　　).
   昨日の横浜，阪神戦はわくわくする試合でした。

2. **a.** We are very (　　　　　　　　　　　　) in Japanese history.
   私たちは日本史に大変興味がある。

   b. The art museum was very (　　　　　　　　　　).
   その美術館は大変興味深かった。

3. **a.** We were (　　　　　　　　　　　) at the news.
   私たちはそのニュースにびっくりしました。

   b. The result of the game was (　　　　　　　　　).
   ゲームの結果は驚くべきものでした。

4. **a.** The audience was (　　　　　　　　　).
   観客は退屈していました。

   b. The movie was (　　　　　　　　).
   その映画は退屈でした。

5. **a.** I was (　　　　　　　　　　　) at his skinny face.
   彼のやつれた顔にショックを受けました。

   b. The news was too (　　　　　　　　　　　) to believe.
   その知らせはあまりにショックで信じられませんでした。

5 (A)〜(D) の 4 つの短い音声を聴き，写真の内容を最も適切に表現しているものを 1 つ選びましょう。

1 (A)　(B)　(C)　(D)

2 (A)　(B)　(C)　(D)

*pupils: 生徒

6 次に読まれる会話文を聴いてその質問に対する応答として最も適切と思われるものを， (A)〜(D) の 4 つの選択肢の中から 1 つ選びましょう。

1 1.　Who was matching whom?　最初の男性の発話をしっかり聞き取ろう！

    (A)　St. Tomas High School vs. St. John High School

    (B)　St. John High School vs. St. Faith High School

    (C)　St. John High School vs. St. King High School

    (D)　St. King High School vs. St. Queen High School

  2.　Were the woman and Thomas classmates in high school?

    (A)　No, they weren't.

    (B)　No, they aren't.

    (C)　Yes, they were.

    (D)　Yes, they are.

2 1.　What will the woman do for a living?

    (A)　She will book a ticket for a show.

    (B)　She will write a book.

    (C)　She will walk to a library.

    (D)　She will arrange the books on the shelves.

  2.　How long does it take to go to the library from the woman's home?

    (A)　It takes about 10 minutes by car.

    (B)　It takes about 10 minutes by train.

    (C)　It takes about 10 minutes' walk.

    (D)　It takes about 10 minutes by bus.

7A （　）に適切な日本語を入れて，英会話文を日本語に直しましょう。

Tom: How many classes do you have on Friday, Mike?

Mike: Two classes, English Literature and American History.

Tom: I have English Literature, too. Mr. Iwamura's last lesson was boring. What was wrong with him?

Mike: He is a big fan of the Mariners, you know. The Mariners have been losing consecutively. Yesterday, the game ended in a 10-1 win for the Yankees.

Judy: Ah, OK. That explains a lot. Wow! You know a lot about baseball.

Mike: Yes. I belonged to the baseball club in junior high school. Did you play any sports, Judy?

Judy: No. I was not good at sports, so I was in the brass band club in junior high and high school. I played the flute in junior high school and the trumpet in high school.

　トム：マイク，金曜日は何コマあるの？

マイク：¹（　　　　　　　　　　　　　　　　　）。英文学と ²（　　　　　　　　　　　　）。

　トム：英文学は僕もとっているよ。³（　　　　　　　　　　　　　　　　　　　　）。
　　　　なんでそうなったんだろう？

マイク：彼はマリナーズの ⁴（　　　　　　　　　　）。知っているだろう。マリナーズは連敗しているんだ。
　　　　昨日，試合はヤンキースが 10 対 1 で勝ったよ。

ジュディ：それでわかったわ。⁵（　　　　　　　　　　　　　）。

マイク：そうだよ。⁶（　　　　　　　　　　　　　　　　）。
　　　　⁷（　　　　　　　　　　　　　），ジュディ？

ジュディ：していないわ。運動は得意じゃなかったの。それで私は ⁸（
　　　　　　　　　　　　　　　　）。中学時代には ⁹（　　　　　　），高校時代には
　　　¹⁰（　　　　　　　　　　　　　　　　）。

7B 次に読まれる英文を聴いてその質問に対する応答として最も適切と思われるものを，
(A)～(D) の 4 つの選択肢の中から 1 つ選びましょう。

1. What do Mr. Iwamura and Mike have in common?
   (A) They study American history.
   (B) They belonged to the brass band club.
   (C) They went to the same junior high school.
   (D) They like baseball.

2. Which musical instrument did Judy play when she was in junior high school?
   (A) Saxophone
   (B) Clarinet
   (C) Trumpet
   (D) Flute

3. What is NOT mentioned in the conversation?
   (A) Mike has two classes on Friday.
   (B) Mike is good at playing the piano.
   (C) The Mariners have not won recently.
   (D) The speakers are university students.

~ *Take a Break* ~

色の認知に違い？

太陽の色は何色でしょうか？「赤」と答える人がほとんどでしょう。日本人が太陽の色は赤いと思い込んでいるのは，国旗の赤い日の丸を太陽の色と思っているからだとの説があります。欧米では太陽を yellow「黄色」で表現するのが一般的です。国によって色彩感覚が違う例として「青リンゴ」は英語で green apple。うっかり blue apple と答えてしまいそうですよね。「青信号」a green light,「芝生は青い」The grass is green. など，日本人は青を green で表現しています。

Unit 4

「道を教えて」の「教えて」は，"teach" だよね？

Q： 日本文に合うように，teach，tell，show のいずれかを（　　）に入れましょう。（15秒）

1.	私に駅までの道を教えてください。	Please (　　　　　　) me the way to the station.
2.	本当のことを教えてください。	(　　　　　　) me the truth.
3.	私に英語を教えてください。	Please (　　　　　　) me English.

上の英文からわかったことは何ですか？自由に書いてみましょう。

Target (　　　　　　　　　　　　　　　　　　　　　　　　　)

1 次の会話文の中に英語の間違えが1つあります。間違えている語に下線を引き，（　　）に適切な英語を書き入れましょう。

> 地図を見ながら図示して教えるときには
> どの動詞を使うかな？

1. John: How can I help you?　どうかしましたか？

   Tomoko: Could you teach me where I am now on this map?

   　　　この地図上のどこにいるのか教えてくれませんか？　　　(　　　　　　　　　)

2. Emi: Hello. This is ABC Company, Emi talking.　もしもし。こちらは ABC 社。恵美です。

   John: May I speak to Noah in the sales department?

   　　　営業部のノアさんをお願いできますか？　　　(　　　　　　　　　)

3. John: Did you say something?　何か言った？

   Naoko: No. I told to myself.　いいえ。独り言を言ったのよ。　(　　　　　　　　　)

4. Sam: Excuse me. Would you mind taking a picture for us?

   　　　すみません。僕たちの写真を撮ってもらえますか？

   Akiko: OK. Stay put. Now, tell "Cheese."

   　　　いいですよ。動かないで。はい，チーズ。　　　(　　　　　　　　　)

5. Joseph: Who is your homeroom teacher?　担任の先生は誰ですか？

   Mari: Mr. Smith. He tells us Japanese.　スミス先生です。彼は私たちに国語を教えています。

   　　　　　　　　　　　　　　　　　　　　　　　(　　　　　　　　　)

2 ( ) から適切な表現を選び○で囲んで，日本文に合う英文を完成させましょう。

1. 銀行への行き方を教えてください。

   Please (tell / teach) me the way to the bank.

2. 彼は地元の学校で地理を教えています。

   He (teaches / tells) *geography at the local school.   *geography: 地理

3. もっとゆっくり話してください。

   Please (say / speak) more slowly.

4. あなたは英語を話すことができますか？

   Can you (speak / talk) English?

5. 彼らはお互いに話す時間がほとんどありません。

   They have little time to (say / talk) to each other.

6. 私たちはグリーン先生からフランス語を教えてもらいます。

   We are (taught / told) French by Mrs. Green.

7. ABC ホテルへの行き方を教えていただけませんか？

   Could you (teach / tell) me the way to the ABC Hotel?

8. 看板に「芝生に入るな」と書いてあります。

   The sign (speaks / says) "Keep off the grass."

9. 彼は私の申し出に「いやだ」と言いました。

   He (said / talked) "No" to my offer.

10. 手紙に彼女は日曜日に着くと書いてあります。

    The letter (speaks / says) she'll arrive on Sunday.

3　（　　）に適切な語を書き入れ，日本文に合う英文を完成させましょう。

1. I (   ) "Good night" to my parents before I go to bed.
   私は寝る前に「おやすみ」と両親に言います。

2. What did you (   )?
   何て言ったの？

3. (On the phone) "May I (   ) to Sam?"
   「サムと話せますか？」

   "(   )".
   「僕です。」

4. (   ) more loudly.
   もっと大きな声で話してください。

5. Please (   ) me the way to the post office.
   郵便局へ行く道を教えてください。

6. Can you (   ) us a little bit about yourself?
   簡単な自己紹介をしてもらえますか？

7. We (   ) on the phone.
   私たちは電話で話しました。

8. When I (   ) to her, we speak to each other in French.
   私は彼女と話すときお互いフランス語で話します。

9. Our English teacher (   ) very well.
   私たちの英語の先生はとても上手に教えてくれます。

10. She (   ) me to play tennis.
    彼女が私にテニスを教えてくれました。

4 (A)～(D) の 4 つの短い音声を聴き，写真の内容を最も適切に表現しているものを 1 つ選びましょう。

1 (A) (B) (C) (D)

2 (A) (B) (C) (D)

5 次に読まれる会話文を聴いてその質問に対する応答として最も適切と思われるものを，(A)～(D) の 4 つの選択肢の中から 1 つ選びましょう。

1 1. Who told the woman some good news?

(A) John

(B) Ted

(C) Mary

(D) Nell

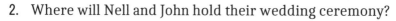

2. Where will Nell and John hold their wedding ceremony?

(A) New York

(B) London

(C) Tokyo

(D) Vancouver

国名をしっかり聞き取ろう！

2 1. Who taught music to the man when he was a high school student?

(A) Mrs. Katayama

(B) Mr. Kato

(C) Mrs. Kawai

(D) Mr. Kitayama

2. What day will the school reunion be held?

(A) Wednesday

(B) Friday

(C) Saturday

(D) Sunday

6A 図表と英文メールを読み，対応する日本語の（　　）に適切な表現を書き入れましょう。

Jade Bagel Shop　FREE BAGEL
Only valid on Tuesday, February 10th
Not to be combined with any other coupons
Limited to one coupon per customer per visit

To: Toshi
From: nyannko@love.com

Hello. Have you gotten used to life in California yet? It's been a month since you came here. Yesterday, you told me that you've never eaten a bagel. I have a coupon. This coupon entitles you to a free bagel at Jade Bagel Shop. This shop is very popular in this town. It is close to my house. Can you come to my house after school? I'll give you the coupon.

Mike

ジェイドベーグルショップ　　¹（　　　　　　　　　　　　　　）
²（　　　　）月 ³（　　　　）日 ⁴（　　　　　　　　　）のみ有効
他のクーポンとは ⁵（　　　　　　　　　　　　）
⁶（　　　　　　　　　　　　）

トシ君へ

From: nyannko@love.com

こんにちは。カルフォルニアの生活には ⁷（　　　　　　　　　　　　　　　）？君がここに来て

⁸（　　　　　　　　　　　　　）。昨日，君は僕に ⁹（　　　　

　　　　）。僕はクーポン券を一枚持っています。この券で君はジェイドベーグルショップのベーグルを

¹⁰（　　　　　　　　　　　）。この店はこの町で ¹¹（　　　　　　　　　　　　　）。

その店は僕の家の近くにあります。¹²（　　　　　　　　　　　　　　）？僕は

¹³（　　　　　　　　　　）。

マイクより

6B 次に読まれる英文を聴いてその質問に対する応答として最も適切と思われるものを，(A)〜(D) の 4 つの選択肢の中から 1 つ選びましょう。 21

> **Jade Bagel Shop   FREE BAGEL**
> Only valid on Tuesday, February 10th
> Not to be combined with any other coupons
> Limited to one coupon per customer per visit

1. Where will Toshi get the coupon?
   (A) At a bagel shop
   (B) At school
   (C) At Mike's house
   (D) At Toshi's house

2. When can you use this coupon?
   (A) Tuesday, February 10th
   (B) Thursday, February 10th
   (C) Tuesday, January 10th
   (D) Thursday, January 10th

3. What is NOT mentioned?
   (A) It's been a month since Toshi came to California.
   (B) Toshi has never eaten a bagel.
   (C) Jade Bagel Shop is very popular.
   (D) Mike has four coupons.

6A に書かれていない文を選ぶ問題だよ！

~ Take a Break ~

Speak or Talk?

皆さんのなかには九官鳥を飼っている方がいらっしゃるかもしれません。「私の九官鳥はしゃべる」を英語に訳すとどうなるでしょうか？ speak は「言葉を発する」ことで talk は「言葉でやりとりする」ということでしたね。「私の九官鳥はしゃべる」は My mynah speaks となりますが，飼い主が九官鳥を会話の相手とみなしている場合には talk を使います。

Unit 5

「このスープ，いい匂い」は "This soup is a good smell." でいいの？

Q: 次の英文で自然な表現は a, b のどちらでしょう？（　　）に○を書き入れましょう。（15秒）

1.	このピザは美味しい。	
	（　　）**a.** This pizza is a good taste.	（　　）**b.** This pizza tastes good.

2.	このスープはひどい臭いです。	
	（　　）**a.** This soup is a bad smell.	（　　）**b.** This soup smells bad.

上の正しい英文からわかったことは何ですか？（　　）に適切な英単語を書き入れましょう。

Target taste や smell は ¹（　　　　）で使うより ²（　　　　　　）で使う方が自然な表現になる。

---

1 次の会話文の中に英語の間違えが1つあります。間違えている語に下線を引き，（　　）に適切な英語を書き入れましょう。

1. John: I'll honk the horn when I get to your house. 家に着いたらクラクションを鳴らすよ。

   Tomoko: OK. I'll hear for it and come running out. 「聞き耳を立てる」は 'listen for' だよ！
   わかった。クラクションの音が聞こえたら走り出て行くわ。（　　　　　　　　）

2. Aki: I see this TV show every week. 私は毎週このテレビ番組を見てるわ。

   John: I love this show. It is funny. その番組大好き。おもしろいよね。

   （　　　　　　　　）

   look forward to 「〜を楽しみにしている」to の後には名詞
   がくるよ。動詞を使いたいときには ing 形（動名詞）にしよう。

3. John: I'm going to come to you. あなたに会いに行くよ。

   Naoko: I'm looking forward to looking you. 会えるのを楽しみにしてるわ。

   （　　　　　　　　）

4. Sam: Hello, Akiko. Nice day, isn't it? こんにちは，明子。いい天気だね。

   Akiko: See at the sky. A beautiful rainbow has appeared.
   空を見て。きれいな虹が出ているわ。　　　　（　　　　　　　　）

5. Joseph: Why are you opening the window? なんで窓を開けているの？

   Mari: The room feels *musty, so I'm airing out the room.
   部屋がカビ臭いので換気をしているのです。　　　　　　　*musty: カビ臭い

   （　　　　　　　　）

2 ( ) から適切な表現を選び○で囲んで，日本文に合う英文を完成させましょう。

1. このドレス似合うかしら？
   How do I (look / see) in my dress?

2. 聞こえますか？
   Can you (listen / hear) me?

3. 見ているだけです。
   I'm just (looking / seeing).

4. えーと。
   Let me (look / see).

5. それはお気の毒ですね。
   I'm sorry to (listen / hear) that.

6. このケーキはすごく甘い。
   The cake (tastes / feels) very sweet.

7. この部屋は煙の臭いがします。
   This room (smells / tastes) smoky.

8. 新しい家で心地がいいです。
   I (taste / feel) comfortable in my new house.

9. 彼は実際より10歳若く見えます。
   He (looks / watches) ten years younger than he is.

10. 私たちはオーケストラを聴く機会がありました。
    We had a chance to (heard / listen) to the orchestra.

3 （　　）に適切な語を書き入れ，日本文に合う英文を完成させましょう。

1. Let's (　　　　　　　　　　　　　) carefully to the dialogue.
   対話を注意深く聞いてみましょう。

2. I (　　　　　　　　　　　　　) that she is in Spain now.
   彼女は今スペインにいるそうです。

3. (　　　　　　　　　　　　　) your step!
   足元に気をつけて！

4. I'm (　　　　　　　　　　　) for a job.
   私は仕事を探しています。

5. I'm glad to (　　　　　　　　　) you.
   お会いできてうれしいです。

6. All of the food (　　　　　　　　　　) good.
   料理はどれもいい味でした。

7. The bath room (　　　　　　　　　　) musty.
   浴室はカビ臭い。

8. I (　　　　　　　　　) lonely.
   私は孤独を感じます。

4 (A)～(D) の 4 つの短い音声を聴き，写真の内容を最も適切に表現しているものを 1 つ選びましょう。

1 (A) (B) (C) (D)

2 (A) (B) (C) (D)

5 次に読まれる会話文を聴いてその質問に対する応答として最も適切と思われるものを， (A)～(D) の 4 つの選択肢の中から 1 つ選びましょう。

1 1. How was the weather last night?

    (A) Fine

    (B) Cloudy

    (C) Terrible

    (D) Sunny

  2. What is NOT mentioned in the dialog?

    (A) Weather

    (B) English lesson

    (C) Coffee

    (D) Thousand

> ダイアローグに出てこない内容を探す問題だよ！

2 1. What will the speakers probably do next Sunday?

    (A) Go to a flower shop

    (B) Enjoy watching the flowers

    (C) Go on a picnic

    (D) Drink some coffee

  2. Where will they meet?

    (A) In the botanical garden

    (B) In front of the botanical garden

    (C) In the book shop

    (D) In front of the book shop

6A （　　　）に適切な日本語を入れて，英会話文を日本語に直しましょう。

Mike: Tom, you look so suntanned. I heard that you went to Okinawa with your parents.

Tom: Yes. The weather was good, and we went diving and surfing.

Mike: Did you try local dishes?

Tom: Yes. One evening, we went to a local restaurant, and it had a live band. We listened to Okinawan music for about thirty minutes and ordered *Mimiga. It looked strange but tasted good.

Mike: Sounds like you had a lot of fun. Was it your first trip to Okinawa?

Tom: No. When I was a junior high school student, I went there on a school trip.

Judy: Tom, did you go shopping? I hope you remembered to buy something for me.

Tom: Yes, of course. I bought a box of sweets. Luckily, I bought one and got one free, so I have one for you and one for your younger sister.

Judy: Oh, thank you so much. I'm sure she will be happy.

Tom: You're welcome.

*Mimiga: 豚の耳を使った沖縄料理の 1 つ

マイク： トム，かなり日焼けしたみたいだね。君は両親と [1]（　　　　　　　　　　　　　）。

トム： ああ。天気がよくてダイビングとサーフィンに行ったんだ。

マイク： [2]（　　　　　　　　　　　）？

トム： 食べたよ。ある晩，僕たちは地元のレストランに行ってそこには生バンド（演奏）があったんだ。 [3]（　　　　　　　　　　　　　　　　） ミミガーを頼んだよ。 [4]（　　　　　　　　　　　　　　）。

マイク： すごく楽しんだようだね。沖縄へは初めて行ったの？

トム： いいや。中学生のときに修学旅行で行ったよ。

ジュディ： トム，買い物には行った？何か買ってきてくれたかしら。

トム： もちろん。お菓子を 1 箱買ったよ。運良く [5]（　　　　　　　　　　　　　）。 1 つは君にそしてもう 1 つは君の妹に。

ジュディ： わー，ありがとう。きっと妹は喜ぶわ。

トム： どういたしまして。

6B 次に読まれる英文を聴いてその質問に対する応答として最も適切と思われるものを，(A)～(D) の 4 つの選択肢の中から 1 つ選びましょう。

1. How many times has Tom been to Okinawa?

   (A) Never

   (B) Once

   (C) Twice

   (D) Three times

2. In Okinawa, what kinds of sports did Tom's family enjoy?

   (A) Indoor sports

   (B) National sports

   (C) Winter sports

   (D) Marine sports

3. Who will get a box of sweets?

   (A) The girl and her sister

   (B) The girl and her friend

   (C) The girl and her parents

   (D) The girl and her brother

 ~ Take a Break ~

Listen or Hear?

このユニットで listen は意識して耳を傾けて「聴く」，hear は意識せず耳に入ってくることを「聞く」ということを学びましたが，「リスニングテスト」,「ヒアリングテスト」はそれぞれどういう時に使いますか？皆さんにお馴染みの「リスニングテスト」は英語の聞き取りテストを指します。流れてくる音声に耳を傾けて積極的に聴かなければならないということですね。一方，「ヒアリングテスト」は耳鼻科などで行われる検査のことです。音が聞こえているかどうかを調べる聴力テストです。

Unit 6 "hard" はどの語を修飾するの？

Q: 次の日本文を参考に文中の（　　）内に入る共通の英単語を書き，その単語がどの単語を説明しているか矢印を書き入れましょう。（10秒）

| 1. | 彼女は働き者です。 | She is a （　　　　）worker. |
| 2. | 彼女はとても一生懸命に働きます。 | She works very （　　　　）. |

上の英文からわかったことは何ですか？自由に書いて見ましょう。

Target （　　　　　　　　　　　　　　　　　　　　　　　　　）

---

1 次の会話文の中に英語の間違えが1つあります。間違えている語に下線を引き，（　　）に適切な英語を書き入れましょう。

1. Cathy: This glass looks so lovely. Can I use it?　このグラスはすごく美しいわ。使ってもいい？

   Takuo: Yes. Please handle it careful.　いいよ。丁寧に扱ってね。

   （　　　　　　　　　　　）

2. Carol: I heard you went on a business trip to Sendai. Wasn't it cold?

   仙台に出張に行ったと聞きました。寒くなかったですか？

   Shinji: It was very cold. We had heavily snow there.　すごく寒かったですよ。大雪でした。

   （　　　　　　　　　　　）

3. Judy: I lived in Paris for two years.　私は2年間パリに住んでいました。

   Takuya: I see. You can speak French very good, can't you?

   なるほど。あなたはフランス語を大変上手に話すことができますからね。

   （　　　　　　　　　　　）

4. Bob: I hate rainy season in Japan. It's so humid.

   日本の梅雨は嫌いだ。すごく蒸し暑い。

   Mariko: Today's weather forecast says it'll rain hardly tomorrow.

   今日の天気予報によれば明日はひどい雨になるよ。　（　　　　　　　　　）

5. John: You bought a new car, didn't you?　新車を買ったんだって？

   Mari: Yes. It's a nice car, and the engine is really quietly.

   ええ。すごくいい車でエンジンが本当に静かなのよ。　（　　　　　　　　　）

2 語群から適切な語を選び（　　）に書き入れ，日本文に合う英文を完成させましょう。
ただし2度使用する語もあります。

careful / carefully / good / hard / hardly /
heavy / heavily / quiet / quietly / well

1. **a.** もっと静かに話してくれませんか。

   Please speak more (　　　　　　　　　).

   b. 図書館の中では静かにしなければなりません。

   You must be (　　　　　　　　　) in the library.

2. **a.** 火の取り扱いに注意しなさい。

   Be (　　　　　　　　　) with the fire.

   b. 私の言うことを注意して聞きなさい。

   Listen to me (　　　　　　　　　).

3. **a.** 君のバッグは重いが僕のは軽い。

   Your bag is (　　　　　　　　　), but mine is light.

   b. 外は激しい雨です。

   It's raining (　　　　　　　　　) outside.

4. **a.** 君は上手に踊るね。

   You are a (　　　　　　　　　) dancer.

   b. 君は上手に踊るね。

   You dance (　　　　　　　　　).

5. **a.** 彼は硬い歯ブラシを使います。

   He uses a (　　　　　　　　　) toothbrush.

   b. トムは必死に笑いをこらえました。

   Tom tried (　　　　　　　　　) not to laugh.

   c. 今ほとんどお金の持ち合わせがありません。

   I have (　　　　　　　　　) any money with me now.

3 1〜8の英語を後半 a〜h と線でつないで，意味を成す英文を完成させましょう。

1. The test was   •   • **a**   the game easily.

2. We won   •   • **b**   is near the library.

3. The bus stop   •   • **c**   easy for me.

4. He is   •   • **d**   nearly sixty.

▶▶ 1〜4で作った英文を日本語に直しましょう。

1. _____

2. _____

3. _____

4. _____

5. These plants grow   •   • **e**   for him to help his old mother.

6. He is   •   • **f**   naturally in this area.

7. It's natural   •   • **g**   a serious mistake.

8. I made   •   • **h**   seriously injured.

▶▶ 5〜8で作った英文を日本語に直しましょう。

5. _____

6. _____

7. _____

8. _____

4 (A)～(D) の 4 つの短い音声を聴き，写真の内容を最も適切に表現しているものを 1 つ選びましょう。

1 (A) (B) (C) (D)

2 (A) (B) (C) (D)

5 次に読まれる会話文を聴いてその質問に対する応答として最も適切と思われるものを，(A)～(D) の 4 つの選択肢の中から 1 つ選びましょう。

1 1. How was the man's last exam?

   (A) He was at the top of the class.

   (B) He will get the 35th of his class this year.

   (C) He did *splendidly on the last exam.

   (D) He did poorly on the last exam.

*splendidly: すばらしく，申し分なく

  2. What will the speakers probably do this weekend?

   (A) Get a bad score

   (B) Have dinner

   (C) Prepare for the exam

   (D) Have a date

2 1. How were the speakers related to each other?

   (A) A teacher and a student

   (B) A doctor and a patient

   (C) Neighbors

   (D) A boss and a *subordinate

*subordinate: 部下

  2. How is the man's life in San Diego?

   (A) Pretty good except for the rent

   (B) Pretty good except for the room

   (C) Pretty good except for the weather

   (D) Pretty good except for the musical noise

6A 図表と英文を読み，対応する日本語の（　　）に適切な表現を書き入れましょう。

Sunlight Café
Open from 7:00 a.m. to 10:00 p.m.

Drinks	Small	Medium	Large	Cakes	
Coffee	$1.00	$1.50	$2.00	Apple cake	$2.00
Tea	$1.00	$1.50	$2.00	Banana cake	$2.00
Apple juice	$1.50	$2.00	$2.50	Chocolate cake	$2.50
Orange juice	$1.50	$2.00	$2.50	Cheesecake	$3.00

All drinks　Get a large for the price of a medium on weekends.

Come to Sunlight Café and fill out a form for a chance to win a trip to Hawaii.

Entry Rules
1. Order something to receive an entry form.
2. Only one entry per person.
3. The closing date is November 30th.
4. The winner will be announced on our homepage.

サンライトカフェ

開店 [1] （　　　　　　　　　　　　　　　　　）

ドリンク	S サイズ	M サイズ	L サイズ	ケーキ	
コーヒー	$1.00	$1.50	$2.00	りんごケーキ	$2.00
紅茶	$1.00	$1.50	$2.00	バナナケーキ	$2.00
アップルジュース	$1.50	$2.00	$2.50	チョコレートケーキ	$2.50
オレンジジュース	$1.50	$2.00	$2.50	チーズケーキ	$3.00

すべての飲み物 [2] （　　　　　　　　　　　　　　　　　）。

今すぐサンライトカフェに来て応募用紙に記入してハワイ旅行を手に入れよう

エントリーのルール

① [3] （　　　　　　　　　　　　　　　　　）何か注文する

② [4] （　　　　　　　　　　　　　　　　　）

③ [5] （　　　　　　　　　　　　　　　　　）

④ [6] （　　　　　　　　　　　　　　　　　）で発表

6B 次に読まれる英文を聴いてその質問に対する応答として最も適切と思われるものを，(A)〜(D) の 4 つの選択肢の中から 1 つ選びましょう。 31

Sunlight Café
Open from 7:00 a.m. to 10:00 p.m.

Drinks	Small	Medium	Large	Cakes	
Coffee	$1.00	$1.50	$2.00	Apple cake	$2.00
Tea	$1.00	$1.50	$2.00	Banana cake	$2.00
Apple juice	$1.50	$2.00	$2.50	Chocolate cake	$2.50
Orange juice	$1.50	$2.00	$2.50	Cheesecake	$3.00

All drinks　Get a large for the price of a medium on weekends.

---

1. How much will you pay when you buy a large-sized tea on Sunday?
   (A) $1.00　　(B) $1.50　　(C) $2.00　　(D) $2.50

2. What should you do at Sunlight Café if you want to go to Hawaii?
   (A) Drink something and get a large-sized tea
   (B) Eat cakes and use a computer
   (C) Go to a travel agency
   (D) Drink something and fill out a form

3. When is the entry deadline?
   (A) The last day of November
   (B) The last day of September
   (C) The last day of December
   (D) The last day of October

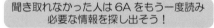
聞き取れなかった人は 6A をもう一度読み
必要な情報を探し出そう！

~ *Take a Break* ~

副詞（adverb）って何？

このユニットで学習した「副詞」は「形容詞」「副詞」「動詞」（＝名詞以外）を修飾する品詞で，主に以下の 5 種類を表します。

「時」　　last night, tomorrow, tonight etc.

「場所」　at school, home, upstair etc.

「程度」　a little, so, too etc.

「頻度」　always, annually, often, yearly etc.

「様態」　carefully, quietly, happily etc.

 以下の文には間違った箇所があります。正しい文に直してみましょう。
I go to there.

Unit 7

「昨夜，怖い夢を見た」って
"I saw a bad dream last night." でいいよね？

Q: 日本文に合うように，get，have，make，take のいずれかを必要であれば適切な形に直し（　　）に入れましょう。（60秒）

1.	人は歳をとるとそんなには寝なくなるものです。 You don't sleep so much when you (　　　　) older.
2.	昨夜，怖い夢を見ました。 I (　　　　) a bad dream last night.
3.	その問題を解決するにはいくらか時間がかかるでしょう。 It'll (　　　　) some time to solve the problem.
4.	音を立てないで。赤ちゃんが寝ています。 Please don't (　　　　) any noise. My baby is sleeping.

上の英文からわかったことは何ですか？（　　）に適切な日本語を入れましょう。

Target 基本的な動詞は（　　　　　　　　　　　　　　　　　　　　　　）ことが大事。

---

1 次の会話文の中に英語の間違えが1つあります。間違えている語に下線を引き，（　　）に適切な英語を書き入れましょう。

1. John: Tomoko, thank you for correcting my mistakes.
   智子，間違いを直してくれてありがとう。

   Tomoko: Well, you often do mistakes when you write a letter in Japanese.
   うーん，あなたは日本語の手紙を書くときによく間違えるよね。（　　　　　　　）

2. Bob: Do you have any daily routine for your health?
   健康のために何かしていることはありますか？

   Miharu: Yes. I usually go a walk in the evening.　ええ。私は普段夕方散歩に行きます。
   （　　　　　　　　　）

3. John: Have you found a new job?　新しい仕事は見つかった？

   Naoko: No, it's difficult to take a new job in a small city.
   いいえ，小さな町で新しい仕事につくのは難しいわ。　（　　　　　　　）

4. Sam: How about going for a drive this afternoon?
   今日の午後にドライブに行くっていうのはどう？

   Akiko: Sounds great. We make the afternoon off.　いいわね。午後は休みだから。
   （　　　　　　　　　）

2 ( ) から適切な表現を選び○で囲んで，日本文に合う英文を完成させましょう。

1. その問題を解決するにはいくらか時間がかかるでしょう。

   It'll (have / take) some time to solve the problem.

2. 息子は時間がなかったので空港までタクシーに乗りました。

   My son (made / took) a taxi to the airport because he had no time.

3. 彼女は母親とあまりうまくいっていません。

   She isn't (getting / having) along very well with her mother.

4. 彼は朝食前にいつもベッドを整えます。

   He always (takes / makes) his bed before breakfast.

5. スミス先生は明日日本文化についてスピーチをする予定です。

   Mr. Smith is going to (make / do) a speech on Japanese culture tomorrow.

6. あなたは 18 歳なのだから車の免許が取れます。

   Now that you are eighteen, you can (get / take) a driver's license.

7. バスで学校に行くのにどれくらいかかりますか？

   How long does it (make / take) to get to school by bus?

8. 私は風邪をひいています。

   I (have / take) a cold.

~ *Take a Break* ~ 答え

there は副詞で「そこへ」という意味で to を入れると「へ」という意味が重複してしまいますので
I go there. が正解となります。（ex: I go to a supermarket. I go there.）

3　（　　）に適切な語を書き入れ，日本文に合う英文を完成させましょう。

1. We're (　　　　　　　　　　　　　　) a party tonight.
   今夜パーティーを開きます。

2. I want to (　　　　　　　　　　　　　　) friends with your sister.
   私はあなたのお姉さんと友達になりたい。

3. It'll (　　　　　　　　　　　　　) some time to solve the problem.
   その問題を解決するにはいくらか時間がかかるでしょう。

4. They did everything in order to (　　　　　　　　　　　　) money.
   彼らは金を儲けるために何でもやりました。

5. My younger brother's condition is (　　　　　　　　　　　) better.
   弟の体調はよくなりつつあります。

6. We (　　　　　　　　　　　　) a good time during our visit to the U.S.
   アメリカ訪問中，私たちは楽しく過ごしました。

7. We (　　　　　　　　　　　　) to Tokyo Station around noon.
   私たちは正午ごろ東京駅に着きました。

8. His doctor advised him to (　　　　　　　　　　　　　) this medicine after
   every meal.
   医者は彼に毎食後この薬を飲むようにアドバイスしました。

9. He asked me to (　　　　　　　　　　　) tea.
   彼は私にお茶を入れるように頼みました。

10. She didn't (　　　　　　　　　　　) my advice, so she remains poor.
    彼女は私の忠告を聞かなかったので，貧しいままです。

4 (A)～(D) の 4 つの短い音声を聴き，写真の内容を最も適切に表現しているものを
1 つ選びましょう。

 1 (A) (B) (C) (D)

 2 (A) (B) (C) (D)

5 次に読まれる会話文を聴いてその質問に対する応答として最も適切と思われるものを，
(A)～(D) の 4 つの選択肢の中から 1 つ選びましょう。

1 1. Where will the man go after school?

*diabetes: 糖尿病

(A) Café

(B) Gym

(C) Hospital

(D) Park

2. What does the man's mother do after meals?

(A) Takes notes

(B) Takes exercise

(C) Takes up jogging

(D) Takes medicine

2 1. Who will make the tea?

(A) The woman

(B) The man

(C) The woman and the man

(D) No one

2. Which country will the man go to on business?

(A) New York

(B) Los Angeles

(C) USA

(D) UK

6A 英文メールを読み，対応する日本語の（　　）に適切な表現を書き入れましょう。

To　　　　Professor Smith <P-smith@homemail.com.>
From　　　Kenichi Ito <S-kenichi@studentmail.com.>
Date　　　October 5, Monday
Subject　　Deadline

ここではレポート提出が遅れるときの
メールに関する問題に挑戦！

Dear Professor Smith,

Hello, My name is Kenichi Ito. I am a first-year student from Japan. I am enrolled in your Basic English II class on Tuesday in the third period. I am sorry, but it is impossible to submit my report on time. I am sick, and I am going to enter the hospital on Tuesday and leave on Friday. Actually, I have a favor to ask you. Is there any chance of your extending the deadline to October 11?

I have one more request to make after leaving hospital. I would like to ask you some questions about the last lecture. Would it be possible to see you next week? Please let me know when you would be available. I would like to take your advice.

I appreciate your consideration very much.

Sincerely,
Kenichi Ito

～へ　　スミス教授 <P-smith@homemail.com.>
～から　伊藤賢一 <S-kenichi@studentmail.com.>
日付　　10 月 5 日 月曜
題名　　1（　　　　　　　　　　）

スミス教授

こんにちは。私は伊藤賢一と申します。日本から来た 1 年生です。2（

　　　　　　　　）。申し訳ありませんが，レポートを期限に提出することができません。具合が悪く，

火曜日に入院して金曜日に退院することになりました。実はお願いがあります。3（

　　　　　　　　　　）？

退院後もう 1 つお願いがあります。4（　　　　　　　　　　　　　　　　　）。来週お会い

できる日がありますか？ご都合がよろしい日を教えてください。ご助言に従いたいと思います。

5（　　　　　　　　　　　　　　　　）。

敬具

伊藤賢一

6B 次に読まれる英文を聴いてその質問に対する応答として最も適切と思われるものを，(A)～(D) の 4 つの選択肢の中から 1 つ選びましょう。

1. The words "enroll in " are closest in meaning to:
    (A) am getting
    (B) am taking
    (C) am having
    (D) am making

2. How many nights will Kenichi stay at the hospital?
    (A) Two
    (B) Three
    (C) Four
    (D) Five

3. What is one of the purposes of the e-mail?
    (A) To take Basic English II
    (B) To ask to extend a deadline
    (C) To go to a bookstore
    (D) To go to a college

~ *Take a Break* ~

Have は意外と難しい

have はもともと「持っている」という意味ですが，この動詞は「状態動詞」としても「動作動詞」としても使うことができます。

「状態動詞」の have	「動作動詞」の have
I have a cold.	I'm having lunch now.

 「物」でも「人」でも「持つ（所有している）状態」であれば have が使えます。次の日本文を英語に直してみましょう。

1. 女は青い目をしています。

2. そのヒーターは * 自動消火機能を備えています。   * 自動消火機能 : automatic fire extinguishing function

Unit 8　否定語をどこに置くの？

Q： 日本語に対応する英語表現として自然な英語は a，b のどちらでしょう？（　　）に〇を書き入れましょう。（30秒）

1.	明日雨が降るといやだなあ。 （　　）**a.** I hope it won't rain tomorrow.　　（　　）**b.** I don't hope it will rain tomorrow.
2.	それはよい考えではないと思います。 （　　）**a.** I think it isn't a good idea.　　（　　）**b.** I don't think it is a good idea.
3.	今日は調子が良くないの。 （　　）**a.** I feel not good today.　　（　　）**b.** I don't feel very good today.
4.	誰も残業をしなかった。 （　　）**a.** None of them worked overtime.　　（　　）**b.** All of them didn't work overtime.

上の 4 つの問題からわかったことは何ですか？（　　）に適切な日本語を入れましょう。

Target　英語の否定語 1（　　　　　　）や 2（　　　　　　）は，日本語でいつも否定表現になるとは限らない。

> 日本語の直訳は，自然な英語にならないときがあるね。

1　次の会話文の中に，あまり自然でない英語の表現が 1 つあります。その表現に下線を引き，（　　）により自然な表現を書き入れましょう。

1.　Judy:　What a relief! I was worried about the problem between you and Kyoko.
　　　　　あ〜よかった！あなたと京子の間の問題について心配していたんだ。
　Takuya:　Hmm, I think it's not easy.　う〜ん，簡単じゃないと思うけど。
　　　　　　　　　　　　　　　　　　　　　　　　（　　　　　　　　　　　）

2.　　Bob:　What's wrong? You look pale.　どうしたの？顔色が悪いよ。
　Mariko:　I feel not good today.　今日は調子が良くないの。（　　　　　　　　　）

3.　Cathy:　Is it OK to tell him?　彼に言っても大丈夫？
　Takako:　Honestly, I can imagine he won't accept my offer.
　　　　　正直，彼が申し出を受け入れるとは想像できないよ。（　　　　　　　　）

4.　Carol:　Have you prepared for tomorrow's school trip?　明日の遠足準備は終わった？
　Shinji:　Yes, I have. I don't hope it will rain tomorrow.
　　　　　うん，終わったよ。明日，雨が降るといやだなあ。　（　　　　　　　）

5.　John:　Something strange was flying high in the sky at midnight again.
　　　　　また，何か奇妙な物が真夜中，空中を飛んでいたよ。
　　Mari:　I believe that wouldn't happen again.　そんなことがまた起こるとは信じられない。
　　　　　　　　　　　　　　　　　　　　　　　　（　　　　　　　　　　　）

2 以下の英文を日本語に直しましょう。

1. I can't imagine he will be able to reach his goal.

   _____

2. I don't feel very good, because I skipped breakfast this morning.

   _____

3. I don't think I have met you before.

   _____

4. I hope you won't follow his advice easily.

   _____

5. I can't believe he would *betray you like that.

   *betray: 裏切る

   _____

3 日本語に対応する英語表現として自然な英語は a，b のどちらでしょう？（　　）に○を書き入れましょう。

1. 彼は来ないと思います。
   いつもと違うスタイルの問題に挑戦してみよう！
   (　　) **a.** I suppose he won't come.
   (　　) **b.** I don't suppose he will come.

2. （残念ながら）ご一緒できないと思います。
   (　　) **a.** I'm afraid that I cannot join you.
   (　　) **b.** I'm not afraid that I can join you.

3. 何か質問はありませんか？
   (　　) **a.** Do you have any questions?
   (　　) **b.** Don't you have any questions?

~ Take a Break ~ 答え

1. She has blue eyes.
2. The heater has an automatic fire extinguishing function.

4. これ以上雨が強くならないといいんですが。
   (   ) **a.** I hope it doesn't rain any harder.
   (   ) **b.** I don't hope it rains any harder.

5. 彼らの誰も残業をしなかった。
   (   ) **a.** All of them didn't work overtime.
   (   ) **b.** None of them worked overtime.

4 1〜5の英語を後半 a〜e と線でつないで，意味を成す英文を完成させましょう。

1. None of them   •   • **a**   he won't make the same mistake.
2. I'm afraid   •   • **b**   joined the party.
3. I don't think   •   • **c**   I can help you.
4. I didn't know   •   • **d**   he married his ex-girlfriend.
5. I hope   •   • **e**   that I can't make it today.

▶▶ 1〜5で作った英文を日本語に直しましょう。

1. _____
2. _____
3. _____
4. _____
5. _____

5 (A)〜(D) の4つの短い音声を聴き，写真の内容を最も適切に表現しているものを1つ選びましょう。

1 (A) (B) (C) (D)

2 (A) (B) (C) (D)

6 次の会話文を読み，その質問に対する応答として最も適切と思われるものを，(A)〜(D) の 4 つの選択肢の中から 1 つ選びましょう。

Cathy: Hey! We don't have Mr. Alex's class today. What are we going to do?

Ken: Let's go to the library to finish the report. Its due date is just around the corner.

Becky: No way! I don't want to do schoolwork. Give me a break.

Ken: How about going to the school cafeteria?

Becky: Come on! I'm already full. And I'm trying to eat less so I won't gain weight.

Cathy: Exercise is the best way to lose weight. So, why don't we go bowling!

Ken: That's a great idea!

Becky: Yeah, couldn't be better! But I'm afraid I don't have any money with me today.

Cathy: That's OK. I'll lend you some. Now, we're on the same page!

1. What made them happy?
   (A) Losing weight
   (B) Having no class
   (C) Finishing the report
   (D) Taking a break

2. Who most likely are the speakers?
   (A) They are co-workers.
   (B) They are part-time workers.
   (C) They are shop assistants.
   (D) They are students at school.

3. Why did Cathy say in the end, "We are on the same page!"?
   (A) They finally decided to go to the school cafeteria.
   (B) They were all reading the same book.
   (C) They reached an agreement.
   (D) They were all happy although they didn't have money.

 ~ Take a Break ~

---

not のあとの省略は何？

否定語 not を含む頻出の会話表現の中に，I'm afraid not. と I hope not. があります。この not は両方「前文の打消し（否定）」を受けています。

1. A: Can you meet me at the city hall?
   B: I'm afraid not. (I'm afraid that I can't meet you at the city hall.) I have an appointment today.
2. A: Miki eats too much. She'll gain weight soon.
   B: Oh, I hope not. (I hope that she won't gain weight soon.)

7A 会話文を読み，対応する日本語の（　　）に適切な表現を書き入れましょう。

1

Tomoko: I don't think we'll make it on time for Mr. Allman's *statistics class.

　Frank: No, I think we can make it. I don't think we'll be late.

Tomoko: Frank, I'm afraid you're too *optimistic.

　Frank: Well, you know me. I like to think positive!

*statistics: 統計学　*optimistic: 楽観的な

　智子：オールマン先生の統計学の授業に ¹（　　　　　　　　　　　　　　　　　　　　）。

フランク：間に合うさ。²（　　　　　　　　　　　　　　　）。

　智子：フランク，あなたは ³（　　　　　　　　　　　　　）じゃないかしら。

フランク：知ってるだろ。僕は ⁴（　　　　　　　　　　　　）！

2

Toshi: I hear Osamu is in hospital. I hope he will get well soon.

Jenny: I hope so, too. However, I got some bad news yesterday. He'll have to
　　　　have a second operation next week.

Toshi: Really? I'm afraid he'll be *depressed.

Jenny: I'm sure he's strong enough to overcome that.

*depressed: 意気消沈した，落ち込んだ

　俊：修が入院中と聞いたけど，¹（　　　　　　　　　　　　　　　）いいんだけれど。

ジェニー：²（　　　　　　　　　　　　　）。だけど，昨日 ³（　　　　　　　　　　　　　　）。

　　　　来週，⁴（　　　　　　　　　　　　　）。

　俊：本当？ ⁵（　　　　　　　　　　　　　　　　　　）。

ジェニー：彼は強いから必ず ⁶（　　　　　　　　　　　　　　）思うよ。

7B 次に読まれる会話文を聴いてその質問に対する応答として最も適切と思われるものを，(A)～(D) の 4 つの選択肢の中から 1 つ選びましょう。 39, 40

1 1. Who is optimistic?

    (A) Tomoko

    (B) Frank

    (C) Both of them

    (D) Neither of them

2. Where most likely are the speakers?

    (A) At a factory

    (B) In a hospital

    (C) In an office

    (D) At school

3. What does the woman think?

    (A) They will skip the class.

    (B) They will lose time.

    (C) They will be late for class.

    (D) They will make mistakes.

2 1. What's the problem with Osamu?

    (A) Trouble with his neighbor

    (B) Severe tooth pain

    (C) Lack of money for a hospital charge

    (D) The next operation

2. What is NOT mentioned?

    (A) They are worried about Osamu.

    (B) Osamu might be depressed.

    (C) They are going to see Osamu in the hospital.

    (D) Yesterday the woman heard some bad news about Osamu.

3. What does the woman think about Osamu?

    (A) He is a strong person.

    (B) He is a weak person.

    (C) He is a morning person.

    (D) He is a coffee person.

Unit 9

「私もよ！」は "too", "either" それとも "neither"？

Q: 日本語に合うように（　　　）に適切な英単語を書き入れましょう。（15秒）

A: How do you like Japanese food?
B: I like sushi very much.
A: Me, ¹(　　　　　　　)！「私もよ！」
B: But honestly, I don't like natto.
A: I knew that. Me, ²(　　　　　　　)！「私もよ！」

上の正解からわかったことは何ですか？自由に書いて見ましょう。

Target (　　　　　　　　　　　　　　　　　　　　　　　　　　　　　)

1 次の会話文の中に英語の間違えが１つあります。間違えている語（句）に下線を引き，（　　　）に適切な英語を書き入れましょう。

1. Debby: I'm making salad for breakfast. Cathy doesn't like tomatoes. How about you?　朝食のサラダを作っているの。キャシーはトマトが好きじゃないのよ。あなたは？
   Mika: I'm sorry. I don't like them, too.　ごめんなさい，私も好きじゃないです。
   (　　　　　　　　　　)

2. John: I'm really full. I don't want to eat any more.
   お腹いっぱいだ。もうこれ以上食べたくないよ。
   Hiroshi Me, too.　僕もだよ。　(　　　　　　　　　　)

3. Dick: They're exchange students from China, aren't they?
   彼らは中国からの留学生ですよね？　　　　　　　　　　　語順に注意！
   Hiro: I think right.　そうだと思いますよ。
   Miki: Umm. I don't think right. = (I think not.)　そうではないと思いますよ。
   (　　　　　　　　　　)

4. Sam: I saw the "Beauty and the Beast" last weekend.　先週末，『美女と野獣』を観たよ。
   Masako: I did so.　私もよ。　(　　　　　　　　　　)

5. Tony: I feel cold. I've caught a bad cold.　寒気がするよ。ひどい風邪をひいちゃったみたい。
   Naoko: I have so. We should stay home from school today.
   私もよ。私たち，今日は学校休んだほうがいいわね。　(　　　　　　　　　　)

6. Riko: I can't stop eating sweets.　甘いものやめれないわ。
   Ann: I can neither. I *have a sweet tooth.　私もよ。甘いものに目がないの。
   (　　　　　　　　　　)
   *have a sweet tooth: 甘党

2 [　　] 内のアルファベットを並び替えて，1 語のいろいろな種類の同意表現を書き入れましょう。

1. A: I think he should consider the theme again.
   B: (Ab　　　　　　　　ly).　　[e u o l s t]

2. A: You made a small mistake here, didn't you?
   B: (Ri　　　　　　　　).　　[g t h]

3. A: She is sure to pass the exam this time.
   B: (De　　　　　　　　ly).　　[t i i e f n]

4. A: I think he's too picky.
   B: (Ex　　　　　　　　ly).　　[c t a]

同意の程度によって
使い分けないとね！

5. A: Tomorrow's concert will be canceled.
   B: (Pr　　　　　　　　ly).　　[b b o a]

3 so と not の内容が詳しくわかるように，次の下線部の応答文を日本語にしましょう。

1. A: Do you think you'll get a promotion this year?
   B: (You are sure you'll get it.) <u>I hope so.</u>

   _____

2. A: Is it going to rain this evening?
   B: (You don't like rain.) <u>I hope not.</u>

   _____

3. A: It's almost nine. Do you have to leave early?
   B: I'm sorry, but <u>I'm afraid so.</u>

   _____

4. A: Can you tell me how to *get in touch with your sister?

   *get in touch with ~ : ～と連絡をとる

   B: <u>I'm afraid not.</u> I don't know where she lives now.

   _____

2と3はいつもと違うスタイルだけど，TOEIC 対応
によく狙われる必須タスクだよ！頑張ってみよう。

(A)〜(D) の 4 つの短い音声を聴き，イラストの内容を最も適切に表現しているものを 1 つ選びましょう。

1 (A) (B) (C) (D)

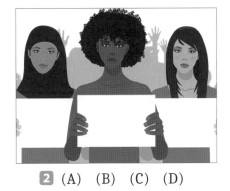

2 (A) (B) (C) (D)

 次に読まれる英文を聴いてその応答として最も適切と思われるものを，(A)〜(D) の 4 つの選択肢の中から 1 つ選びましょう。

1. (A) Probably.
   (B) So can my brother.
   (C) So am I.

2. (A) So did I.
   (B) So do I.
   (C) I hope so.

3. (A) Me, neither.
   (B) I think not.
   (C) Neither am I.

4. (A) Neither did I.
   (B) I didn't, neither.
   (C) So did I.

6 次に読まれる会話文を聴いてその質問に対する応答として最も適切と思われるものを，(A)～(D) の４つの選択肢の中から１つ選びましょう。 44

1. Where did the man go to?
    (A) A dance party
    (B) A movie theater
    (C) A live concert
    (D) A musical performance

2. How were the reviews?
    (A) Fairly good
    (B) Not bad
    (C) Not good
    (D) Terrible

3. According to the conversation, which is probably true?
    (A) The woman wants to go to the concert, too.
    (B) The woman won't buy a ticket for the same concert.
    (C) The man didn't have a good impression of the concert last night. Some critics didn't, either.
    (D) The man was disappointed because of the bad weather.

7A　（　　　）に適切な日本語を入れて，英会話文を日本語に直しましょう。

John: Hi, Keiko. Hi, Satoshi. What's up? You both look a little down today.

Keiko: I haven't finished my report for physics class.

Satoshi: Really? Me, neither!

John: Are you going to today's class?

Keiko: No, I'm not. I don't want to go because I've had a bad headache since last night. How about you, Satoshi?

Satoshi: Neither am I. But you know today is the deadline of the report.

Keiko: I know. We had better go to the class and explain the reason why we can't submit our reports today. What do you think, John?

John: I think so, too. That's the best way to avoid giving him a bad impression of you both.

Keiko & Satoshi: Absolutely! "Honesty is the best policy" is our motto.

ジョン：啓子と智，どうしたの？二人とも今日は，¹（　　　　　　　　　　　　　　　　　　　）。

啓子：物理学のレポートがまだ終わっていないの。

智：本当？²（　　　　　　　　　　）！

ジョン：今日の授業に行くかい？

啓子：³（　　　　　　　　　）昨夜からずっと頭痛で行きたくないの。智は？

智：⁴（　　　　　　　　）。けど，今日はレポートの締め切り日だよ。

啓子：知ってるわ。授業に行って，⁵（　　　　　　　　　　　　　　　）説明するべきよ。ジョン，どう思う？

ジョン：⁶（　　　　　　　　　）。それが，君たちの⁷（　　　　　　　　　　）一番の方法だよ。

啓子＆智：⁸（　　　　　　　　　）！「⁹（　　　　　　　　　　　　）」が私たちのモットーさ。

7B 次に読まれる会話文を聴いてその質問に対する応答として最も適切と思われるものを、(A)〜(D) の４つの選択肢の中から１つ選びましょう。

1. What's the reason why Keiko doesn't want to go to physics class?
   - (A) She has a bad cold.
   - (B) She has a bad headache.
   - (C) She feels sick.
   - (D) She's lazy.

2. What will John probably say next?
   - (A) How about taking a break at a café?
   - (B) Let's go to class together.
   - (C) Let's skip the class together.
   - (D) Both of you should get counseling.

3. What are two of them going to do?
   - (A) Finish their reports
   - (B) Submit their reports to their teacher
   - (C) Go to see a doctor
   - (D) Apologize to the teacher and explain

~ *Take a Break* ~

同意表現ってこんなにあるの！

このユニットで扱った同意表現, Me, too. や Me, neither. などは、会話をスムーズに進める「同意の相槌」となります。感情を相手にわかりやすく伝えることが習慣でない日本人は、このような「あなたのお話をちゃんと聞いていますよ」ということを言葉で表すのが苦手かもしれません。しかし、日本人は英語を話しだした途端に、Really? や Yes, yes, yes. を連発しすぎ！とよくいわれます。気をつけたいですね。

シチュエーション別：いろいろな「相槌」表現
音声に続いて照れずにイントネーションを上手に真似てみましょう

1. That's cool.   That's fantastic.   That's wonderful!
2. You're right.   Exactly!
3. Are you?   Do you?   Is it?
4. Oh, my.   No way!
5. Ah-huh.   Mm-hm.
6. That's too bad.   Are you kidding?   Are you serious?   How awful.   Terrible!

Unit 10　「〜がある・いる」は英語でどう表現するの？

Q: 日本語とうまく対応していない英文はどれでしょう？（　　）に×を入れましょう。（60秒）

1.	（　）	テーブルの上に私のカバンが**ある**。 There is my bag on the table.
2.	（　）	テーブルの上にカバンが1つ**ある**。 There is a bag on the table.
3.	（　）	あそこに空席が2つ**ある**。 There are two empty seats over there.
4.	（　）	銀行の前に本屋が**ある**。 There is a bookstore in front of the bank.
5.	（　）	銀行の前に紀伊国屋書店が**ある**。 There is Kinokuniya bookstore in front of the bank.

上の正しい英文からわかったことは何ですか？自由に書いてみましょう。

Target　（　　　　　　　　　　　　　　　　　　　　　　　　　　　　）

---

1 次の会話文の中に英語の間違えがあります。間違えている表現に下線を引き，（　　）に適切な英語を書き入れましょう。

1.　Tony:　Can you see any difference between these two?
　　　　　　これら2つの違いがわかりますか？

　Junko:　Wait a minute. Ah, a big difference is there.
　　　　　　ちょっと待って。あ，大きな違いがあります。

　　　　　（　　　　　　　　　　　　　　　　　　　　　　　　　）

2.　Bob:　Miki, do you know where Meg's smartphone is?　美樹, メグの携帯知らない？

　Miki:　Well, I saw it before…. Ah, I remember now! There was her smart phone on the shelf by the sink.
　　　　　えっと，どこかで見たわ……。あ，思い出した！彼女の携帯は洗面所の棚にあったわよ。

　　　　　（　　　　　　　　　　　　　　　　　　　　　　　　　）

3.　Meg:　Kenta, how was the party last night?　健太, 昨夜のパーティーはどうだった？

　Kenta:　There was a funny happening at the end of the party.
　　　　　　パーティーの最後に，おもしろいハプニングがあったんだ。

　　　　　（　　　　　　　　　　　　　　　　　　　　　　　　　）

2 以下の英文の正しいものに○，間違っているものに×を（　　）に記入しましょう。

1. （　）　There is a paper cup under the table.

2. （　）　The paper cup is under the table.

3. （　）　There are my brothers in the living room.

4. （　）　My brothers are in the living room.

5. （　）　There was some wine to taste while eating the food.

6. （　）　There are a lot of information about the matter.

7. （　）　There were no free tables at the bar.

8. （　）　*Cultural differences were there.

9. （　）　There are cultural differences between them.

*cultural differences: 文化的差異

3 There is/are/will be のどれかを下線部に書き，英文を完成させましょう。

1. _____ a lot of accidents on this road.

2. Look! _____ a beautiful rainbow in the sky.

3. _____ five players on a basketball team.

4. When you arrive at the airport, _____ *someone to meet you.

*someone: 誰か

5. _____ a non-stop flight at 11 a.m.

6. _____ too much salt in this soup.

ここでしっかり基本をおさえよう！

4 Is/Are there か There isn't/aren't のどちらかを下線部に書き，英文を完成させましょう。

1. _____ eight planets in the solar system?—Yes, there are.

2. Excuse me, _____ a supermarket near here?—No, there isn't.

3. How many students _____ in the class?—Thirty-four.

4. That's too bad. _____ any chairs to sit on in this room?

5. _____ any information about the *political situation?
—No. Nothing yet. *political situation: 政局，政治情勢

6. _____ nothing wrong with her.

5 [　]内の英単語を正しく並び替えて，日本語に合う英文を完成させましょう。
ただし文頭にくる語も小文字で示してあります。

1. そのネコはソファーの上にいます。
[is / the sofa / the cat / on].

_____

2. ソファーの上にネコが一匹います。
[a cat / is / on / there / the sofa].

_____

3. デパートの向かいに紀伊国屋書店があります。 *across from: ～の向かいに
[across from / the department store / is / Kinokuniya bookstore].

_____

4. デパートの向かいに書店があります。
[a bookstore / the department store / is / across from / there].

_____

5. 私の家の周りにはたくさんの自然がある。
[my house / a lot of trees / are / around / there / and fields].

_____

6. この道路は交通量が多い。
[on / a lot of traffic / there / this road / is]. *a lot of traffic: 多くの交通量

_____

6 (A)〜(D) の 4 つの短い音声を聴き，写真の内容を最も適切に表現しているものを 1 つ選びましょう。

1 (A)　(B)　(C)　(D)

2 (A)　(B)　(C)　(D)

7 次の質問文を聴いて，最も適切と思われる応答文を (A)〜(C) の 3 つの選択肢の中から 1 つ選びましょう。

1.　(A)　(B)　(C)

2.　(A)　(B)　(C)

3.　(A)　(B)　(C)

4.　(A)　(B)　(C)

8A　広告文を読み，対応する日本語の（　　）に適切な表現を書き入れましょう。

A Flea Market at Green Park!

There is a flea market at Green Park next Sunday, March 8th. It will start at 10 a.m. and end at 3 p.m.

Are there unnecessary things in your home? If there are, why don't you bring them to our flea market? You can bring anything you won't need any more, like books, clothes, toys, kitchen *appliances, *furniture and so on, as long as they are clean and usable. And if you're lucky, you might be able to find something you've been wanting.

Please understand, we ask that you take all unsold goods back to your home.

P.S.: On that day, there will be a street performance at the flea market. We kindly ask you to refrain from using your cars because *congestion is expected.

*appliance: 器具，道具　*furniture: 家具　*congestion:（交通などの）混雑

グリーンパークでの「蚤の市」

来週の日曜日 3 月 8 日に，¹（　　　　　　　　　　　　　　　　　　　）。午前 10 時から
午後 3 時までです。

²（　　　　　　　　　　　　　　　）？もしあるなら，それらを「蚤の市」に持って
³（　　　　　　　　　　　　　　　）？清潔で使用可能であれば，もう必要のないもの，
本・洋服・おもちゃ・台所用品・家具など，
⁴（　　　　　　　　　　　　　　　）。また，もし運が良ければ，
⁵（　　　　　　　　　　　　　　　）見つかるでしょう。

⁶（　　　　　　　　　　　　　　　）ものにつきましては，家にお持ち帰りいただくことを
どうぞご理解ください。

P.S. 当日「蚤の市」で，大道芸（ストリートパフォーマンス）があります。混雑が予想されますので，
⁷（　　　　　　　　　　　　　　　）。

8B 次に読まれる広告文を聴いてその質問に対する応答として最も適切と思われるものを，(A)〜(D) の４つの選択肢の中から１つ選びましょう。

1. What's the main purpose of this *leaflet?   *leaflet: (広告の) ちらし

   (A) A live performance

   (B) A flea market

   (C) Notice of traffic congestion

   (D) A free market

2. What are you expected to bring?

   (A) Your favorite things

   (B) Your cars

   (C) Anything you want to buy

   (D) Any unnecessary things that you want to sell

3. What are they asking *participants to do?   *participant: 参加者

   (A) Do performance

   (B) Sell necessary goods

   (C) Visit or sell things at the flea market

   (D) Take unsold goods to the flea market

 ~ Take a Break ~

「There 構文」っていろいろあるよ！

「There 構文」の応用として，助動詞（will / might / should）や婉曲（seem）表現を含む文があります。各ニュアンスの違いを確認しておきましょう。

  1. There <u>will</u> be a large *attendance at the meeting.「〜だろう」   *attendance: 出席者

  2. There <u>might</u> be a large attendance at the meeting.「ひょっとしたら〜かも」

  3. There <u>should</u> be a large attendance at the meeting.「〜のはず」

  4. There <u>seems</u> to be a large attendance at the meeting.「〜のようだ」

また，「There 構文」には be 動詞だけでなく，live, stand, come などもよく使われるので覚えておきましょう。

  5. There <u>lived</u> a beautiful woman in the wood.

  6. There <u>stands</u> a church on the hill.

  7. There may <u>come</u> a day when our cars are replaced with self-driving cars.

Unit 11

「私は自転車を盗まれた」は "I was stolen my bike." でいいの？

Q: 日本語に対応する英語表現として自然な英語は a，b のどちらでしょう？（　　）に○を書き入れましょう。（40 秒）

1.	私は自転車を盗まれた。 （　）**a.** I was stolen my bike.　　　（　）**b.** I had my bike stolen.
2.	私は，授業中スマートフォンを使用して先生に叱られた。 （　）**a.** My teacher yelled at me for using a smartphone during the class. （　）**b.** I was scolded for using a smartphone during the class.
3.	この小説は，去年よく売れた。 （　）**a.** This novel was sold well last year.　（　）**b.** This novel sold well last year.

上の正解からわかったことは何ですか？自由に書いてみましょう。

Target （　　　　　　　　　　　　　　　　　　　　　　　　）

1 次の英文の中に，自然でない英語の表現があります。その表現に下線を引き，（　　）により自然な表現を書き入れましょう。

1. This meat is cut very easily with this knife.

　　　この肉はこのナイフでとても簡単に切れる。　　　　　　　（　　　　　　　　　）

2. This fabric is washed well.

　　　この生地はよく洗濯がきく。　　　　　　　　　　　　　　（　　　　　　　　　）

3. Kate dressed in a yellow sleeveless dress at yesterday's party.

　　　ケイトは昨日のパーティーでノースリーブの黄色いワンピースを着ていた。（　　　　　　　　　）

4. Thirty people injured in the accident.

　　　その事故で 30 人の人々が負傷した。　　　　　　　　　　（　　　　　　　　　）

5. The train crowded with high school students.

　　　列車は高校生でいっぱいだった。　　　　　　　　　　　　（　　　　　　　　　）

6. I caught in a shower on my way to school.

　　　学校へ行く途中でにわか雨にあいました。　　　　　　　　（　　　　　　　　　）

英語って不思議～？

2 語群から適切な語（句）を選び（　　　）に書き入れ，日本文に合う英文を完成させましょう。

> caught / were caught / crowded / is crowded / cuts / is cut
> dressed / was dressed / injured / were injured
> wash / are washed / had her bag stolen / was stolen her bag

1. 雨降りの日はバスは混んでいます。
   The bus (　　　　　　　　　　　　　) on rainy days.

2. 私たちは放課後，夕立にあいました。
   We (　　　　　　　　　　) in an evening shower after school.

3. チーズはナイフでたやすく切れる。
   Cheese (　　　　　　　　　) easily with a knife.

4. 交通事故で数人の乗客が負傷した。
   A few passengers (　　　　　　　　　　　) in the traffic accident.

5. このナイロンの靴下は洗濯がききます。
   These nylon socks (　　　　　　　　　) well.

6. 彼女は赤いセーターを着ていた。
   She (　　　　　　　　　) in a red sweater.

7. 母は外出中にバッグを盗まれました。
   My mother (　　　　　　　　　　　) while she was out.

> 次の問題で「受動態」の英文の意味を
> さらに深く理解しよう！

3 以下の英文は受動態を含みますが，その和訳は一般的に能動態で表します。
【例】にならって，（　　　）に日本語を書き和訳を完成させましょう。

【例】 The main office is located in Chicago, USA.
本社はアメリカの（　　　　シカゴにあります　　　　）。

1. Tables are *neatly arranged in each room.   *neatly: きちんと
   テーブルはそれぞれの部屋に（　　　　　　　　　　　　　　　）。

2. The meeting rooms were all occupied, so we went out of the office.
   会議室は（　　　　　　　　　　　　　　　），私たちはオフィスを出た。

3. The flight <u>was delayed</u> due to mechanical problems.

   私の飛行機は （   ）。

4. James Dean <u>was killed</u> in a car accident in 1955.

   ジェームスディーンは 1955 年に （   ）。

5. You're <u>supposed</u> to spend Christmas with your family.

   あなたはクリスマスを （   ）。

6. My brother <u>is dressed</u> in yellow striped-shirt today.

   今日，兄は黄色いストライプのシャツを （   ）。

4 1 ～ 7 の英語を後半 a ～ g と線でつないで，意味を成す英文を完成させましょう。

1. Visitors are   ・   ・ a   occupied now.

2. John was   ・   ・ b   supposed to register at the front desk.

3. The 8:30 train is   ・   ・ c   *alphabetically arranged.

4. The bathroom is   ・   ・ d   delayed about fifteen minutes.

5. The files are   ・   ・ e   killed in a car crash.

6. The Japanese actress was ・   ・ f   stolen while she was out.

7. Her bag was   ・   ・ g   dressed in kimono.

*alphabetically: アルファベット順に

▶▶ 1 ～ 7 で作った英文を日本語に直しましょう。

1. _____

2. _____

3. _____

4. _____

5. _____

6. _____

7. _____

5 例にならって下線部を日本語に直しましょう。

TOEIC の写真問題では解答選択肢として，進行形の英文がよく使用されるよ。その中には受動態の英文も含まれるよ！

進行形＋受動態＝ be 動詞＋ being ＋過去分詞形
The new protein supplement is being advertised on the Net.
広告中です

---

1. Our school is being built behind the hill.　　　（　　　　　　　）

2. The air conditioner is being repaired.　　　　（　　　　　　　）

3. The meeting room is being used.　　　　　　（　　　　　　　）

4. The tire is being filled in the garage.　　　　　（　　　　　　　）

5. The trees are being cut down by the man.　　　（　　　　　　　）

6. The plants are being trimmed.　　　　　　　（　　　　　　　）

7. The car is being washed.　　　　　　　　　（　　　　　　　）

そうだったのね～，納得！

　~ Take a Break ~

"It can't be helped." はどういう意味？

受動態（be 動詞＋動詞・過去分詞形）を含む会話表現 It can't be helped. は直訳すると「それは助けられない，助けられることができない」になります。一方，日本語ではよく「仕方ない，しょうがない」と訳されています。しかし，この訳のニュアンスと実際の英語には，少し意味のズレがあります。これは日本語で「どうしようもない，他に選択肢がない」というような少し切迫感を含んだ表現です。

それもそのはず！ここで使われている help は「助ける」ではなく，「避ける」という語義から来ています。これなら It can't be helped. の持つ本来の意味がよく理解できますね。

6 (A)〜(D) の 4 つの短い音声を聴き，写真の内容を最も適切に表現しているものを
1 つ選びましょう。

(51, 52)

1 (A) (B) (C) (D)   **2** (A) (B) (C) (D)

 7 次に読まれる会話文を聴いてその質問に対する応答として最も適切と思われるものを，
(A)〜(D) の 4 つの選択肢の中から 1 つ選びましょう。

53

1. What are the speakers talking about?
   (A) Rollar coasters at Tokyo Disneyland
   (B) Weekend schedule
   (C) Chiba prefecture
   (D) Slow season

2. What does the woman want to do with the man?
   (A) Stay at home
   (B) Go out for dinner
   (C) Clean up her room
   (D) Go to a theme park

3. What is probably NOT correct about the man?
   (A) He doesn't like taking the initiative.
   (B) He doesn't like going out with the woman.
   (C) He doesn't like crowded amusement parks very much.
   (D) He doesn't like going out on weekends.

8　グラフを見て，その質問に対する応答として最も適切と思われるものを，(A)〜(D) の 4 つの選択肢の中から 1 つ選びましょう。

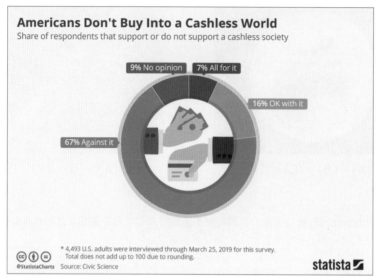

出典：https://www.statista.com/chart/17667/support-of-cashless-payments-united-states/

1. What is the main purpose of the research?
   (A) To know which generations prefer a cashless system
   (B) To know why American people agree to a cashless society
   (C) To know whether American people approve of a cashless society
   (D) To know when a cashless society started in the U.S.

2. Which can be *plausibly said according to the results of the survey?
   (A) A lot of people prefer to use cards to cash.
   (B) A lot of people are eager to *embrace a cashless society.
   (C) A lot of people seem to have some problems about using cards.
   (D) In every state, the number of cashless shops will drastically increase.

   *plausibly: もっともらしく　*embrace: 〜を採用する，〜に喜んで応じる

3. What share of people in the U.S. didn't have an opinion on whether having a cashless society would be a good thing or not.
   (A) Under a tenth
   (B) About a third
   (C) Almost a quarter
   (D) It doesn't say.

Unit 12

似たような単語ばかり……
いったいどれを選べばいいの？

Q1： 最も適切な英単語を選択肢から選びましょう。（15秒）

1.	A new pair of glasses (　　　　　) nice. (A) be 　　　 (B) am 　　　 (C) is 　　　 (D) are
2.	Each of my neighbors (　　　　　) two cars now. (A) has 　　　 (B) have 　　　 (C) having 　　　 (D) had

上の2つの問題からわかったことは何ですか？次の（　　　）に適切な日本語を入れましょう。

Target TOEIC の語彙問題で正解を出すには，（　　　　　　　　　　　　　　）の知識が必要だ。

上にならって以下の問題を解き，完成した英文を日本語に直しましょう。

1. The fashion show ------- in December every year.

    (A) took place   (B) taking place   (C) takes place   (D) have taken

    _____

2. Phonetics ------- the study of speech sounds.

    (A) is   (B) are   (C) was   (D) were

    _____

3. Each of our *valued customers ------- us more motivated all the time.

    *valued customers: 大切な顧客

    (A) make   (B) makes   (C) is made   (D) are making

    _____

TOEIC 対策・特化スタイルユニット。
この分野をマスターして得点アップを目指そう！

Q2: 最も適切な英単語を選択肢から選びましょう。（15 秒）

1.	After the message (　　　　　), some errors occurred on the smartphone. (A) send out　　(B) sent out　　(C) is sent out　　(D) was sent out			
2.	Tourists are (　　　　　) to stay in their rooms after 9 p.m. (A) require　　(B) requires　　(C) requiring　　(D) required			

上の 2 つの問題からわかったことは何ですか？次の（　　　）に適切な日本語を入れましょう。

Target　TOEIC の語彙問題で正解を出すには（　　　　　　　　　　　　　　）の知識が必要だ。

上にならって以下の問題を解き，完成した英文を日本語に直しましょう。

1. My parents ------- to their wedding reception.

　　(A) invited　　　　(B) will invite　　　(C) were invited　　(D) were inviting

　　_____

2. Any problems with the computer system should ------- to the supervisor.

　　(A) report　　(B) have reported　　(C) be reported　　(D) has been reported

　　_____

3. A marketing strategy should ------- current market research.

　　(A) be based　　　(B) be based on　　(C) base on　　　(D) been based on

　　_____

Q3: 最も適切な英単語を選択肢から選びましょう。（15 秒）

1.	I'd rather explain it to (　　　　　) as they're very confused. (A) they　　(B) their　　(C) them　　(D) theirs			
2.	The company is *facing challenges due to (　　　　　) *continuous budget deficits. (A) it　　　(B) it's　　　(C) its　　　(D) them <div align="right">*face: 〜に直面する　continuous budget deficits: 継続する予算不足</div>			

上の 2 つの問題からわかったことは何ですか？次の（　　　）に適切な日本語を入れましょう。

Target　TOEIC の語彙問題で正解を出すには，（　　　　　　　　　　　　　）の知識が必要だ。

上にならって以下の問題を解き，完成した英文を日本語に直しましょう。

1. The woman told the children to divide all the fruits among ------- .

　　(A) herself　　　　(B) itself　　　　(C) themselves　　(D) ourselves

　　_____

2. To whom it may concern: Please make sure that all the doors are closed when
   ------- leave the room.

   (A) you   (B) your   (C) yours   (D) yourself

3. She carelessly dropped her handmade doll and stepped on ------- body.

   (A) it   (B) they   (C) them   (D) its

適当な意味だけの知識は間違えのもと！

Q4: 最も適切な英単語を選択肢から選びましょう。（15 秒）

1.	He was so attracted by her (　　　　) that he sent a letter to her. (A) beautify　　(B) beautifully　　(C) beauty　　(D) beautiful
2.	Our teacher always advises us to speak (　　　　) to the audience during presentations. (A) slowness　　(B) slowly　　(C) slow　　(D) slowing

上の 2 つの問題からわかったことは何ですか？次の（　　　）に適切な日本語を入れましょう。

Target　TOEIC の語彙問題で正解を出すには，単語の意味だけではなく正確な（　　　　　　　）
の知識（修飾関係）が必要だ。

上にならって以下の問題を解き，完成した英文を日本語に直しましょう。

1. Mike gave his girlfriend ------- diamond ring last night.

   (A) an extremely expensive   (B) extremely an expensive
   (C) a extremely expensive   (D) an expensive extremely

2. Tim has many female friends but ------- more.

   (A) want still   (B) wants still   (C) still wants   (D) still want

3. Mr. Tanabe included colorful graphs in his presentation to *ensure that his
   points were ------- understood.   *ensure: 〜を確実にする，〜だと確信する

   (A) clear   (B) clearly   (C) clearness   (D) clearing

前置詞・接続詞の違いは大丈夫？

Q5: 最も適切な英単語を選択肢から選びましょう。（15秒）

1.	(　　　　　) many problems, they were finally able to reach the goal. (A) Though　　　(B) Because　　　(C) However　　　(D) Despite
2.	I'd like to know (　　　　) he's getting along with his new roommate. (A) that's　　　(B) if　　　(C) however　　　(D) even though

上の2つの問題からわかったことは何ですか？次の（　　　）に適切な日本語を入れましょう。

Target TOEIC の語彙問題で正解を出すには，（　　　　　　　　　　　　）の知識が必要だ。

上にならって以下の問題を解き，完成した英文を日本語に直しましょう。

1. The package wasn't delivered ------- the following reasons.

　　(A) because　　　(B) due to　　　(C) as　　　(D) with

　　_____

2. More people have started suffering ------- allergies this spring.

　　(A) from　　　(B) on　　　(C) to　　　(D) for

　　_____

3. ------- conflict of opinions was inevitable, the MC of the symposium *gave up

　　on discussing the matter.　　　　　　　　　　　　　　*give up on: 断念する

　　(A) While　　　(B) Even though　　　(C) Because　　　(D) If

　　_____

さあ，あともう一息，Keep on going!

Q6: 最も適切な英単語を選択肢から選びましょう。（15秒）

1.	A new pair of shoes (　　　　) nice. (A) be　　(B) am　　(C) is　　(D) are
2.	Tourists enjoyed (　　　　) a great beach view from the balcony. (A) see　　(B) saw　　(C) seeing　　(D) seen

上の2つの問題からわかったことは何ですか？次の（　　　）に適切な日本語を入れましょう。

Target TOEIC の語彙問題で正解を出すには，（　　　　　　　　　　　　）の知識が必要だ。

上にならって以下の問題を解き，完成した英文を日本語に直しましょう。

1. My son has started to consider ------- his career due to an economic boom.

　　(A) change　　　(B) to change　　　(C) changed　　　(D) changing

　　_____

2. The shop refused ------- his money as ten days had already passed since the purchase.

    (A) *refund   (B) to refund   (C) refunded   (D) refunding

                                                    *refund: 〜を払い戻す

3. Ms. Ishii has detailed knowledge of teaching, ------- worked in the school for over 30 years.

    (A) has   (B) have   (C) having   (D) had

「人を使って何かのお役を
してもらう」と覚えよう！

Q7: 最も適切な英単語を選択肢から選びましょう。（20秒）

1.	I should have my hair (　　　　　) by this Thursday for the job interview. 　(A) cut　　　　(B) to cut　　　　(C) cuts　　　　(D) cutting
2.	My mother often has her office (　　　　　) because of her busy schedule. 　(A) clean　　　(B) to clean　　　(C) cleaned　　　(D) leaning

上の2つの問題からわかったことは何ですか？次の（　　　）に適切な日本語を入れましょう。

Target　TOEIC の語彙問題で正解を出すには，（　　　　　　　　　　　　）の知識が必要だ。

上にならって以下の問題を解き，完成した英文を日本語に直しましょう。

1. My sister often made me ------- her shirts.

    (A) *iron   (B) to iron   (C) ironing   (D) ironed

                                                    *iron: アイロンをかける

2. We have to get the copy machine ------- .

    (A) repair   (B) to repair   (C) repairing   (D) repaired

3. We have the fire-safety officer ------- the building every month as a safety precaution.

    (A) inspects   (B) inspect   (C) inspected   (D) to inspected

Q8: 最も適切な英単語を選択肢から選びましょう。（20秒）

1.	I wish I ( ) her email address. (A) know (B) knew (C) known (D) knows
2.	If I had known her email address, I ( ) her. (A) email (B) emailed (C) have emailed (D) could have emailed

上の2つの問題からわかったことは何ですか？次の（　　　）に適切な日本語を入れましょう。

Target TOEIC の語彙問題で正解を出すには，（　　　　　　　　　　　　　）の知識が必要だ。

上にならって以下の問題を解き，完成した英文を日本語に直しましょう。

1. If there were a lot more profit this term, *employees ------- an extra bonus.

    *employee: 従業員

    (A) acquire   (B) acquired   (C) will acquire   (D) would acquire

    _____

2. Had the manager informed *the General Affairs Department of our complaint, he ------- *fired.

    *the General Affairs Department: 総務部   *fire: 解雇する

    (A) wasn't   (B) wouldn't been   (C) won't been   (D) wouldn't have been

    _____

3. If you ------- your boss' advice, you could have a managerial position now.

    (A) take   (B) have taken   (C) had taken   (D) took

    _____

「もし〜なら……。」ではなく，
「事実と反すること」が仮定法！

Unit 13 いろいろなタイプの疑問文にどう答える？
—Yes-No 疑問文なのに Yes / No で答えないの？

Q: 質問文に対する適切な応答文はどれでしょうか。（20 秒）

1.	A: Is there a good café nearby? B: （　　）(A) Yes, I have. 　　（　　）(B) Are you new here? 　　（　　）(C) Don't mention it.
2.	A: Are you going to visit Ottawa this month? B: （　　）(A) Sure. It's my pleasure. 　　（　　）(B) No, you're going to a new cinema. 　　（　　）(C) I've already booked a hotel.

TOEIC でよく狙われる！

上の 2 つの問題からわかったことは何ですか？自由に書いてみましょう。

Target （　　　　　　　　　　　　　　　　　　　　　　　　　　）

---

1 次の会話文の応答文として最も適切と思われるものを，(A)〜(C) の 3 つの選択肢の中から 1 つ選びましょう。

1. A: Do you know where I can get a concert ticket?
   B: (A) I'm not sure.
   　　(B) No, I can't.
   　　(C) Maybe you can.

2. A: May I use this computer?
   B: (A) Why can't you?
   　　(B) Sure, go ahead.
   　　(C) How many do you need?

3. A: Would you like something to eat?
   B: (A) Yes. No problem.
   　　(B) It's a good one.
   　　(C) I'm not hungry, thanks.

4. A: Do you mind if I smoke?
   B: (A) Not at all.
   　　 (B) That's what I said.
   　　 (C) Let me make sure.

5. A: Will they refund your money?
   B: (A) I like your refined manners.
   　　 (B) Yes, I'll find it.
   　　 (C) I think they will.

2 　語群から疑問詞を含む適切な句を選び（　　　　）に書き入れ, 日本文に合う英文を完成させましょう。

> how far / how long / how many / how much
> why don't you / why don't we

1. ジェフはどれくらいその店で働く予定ですか？
   (　　　　　　　　　　　　　　) is Jeff going to work at the shop?

2. JR の駅からあなたの家までどのくらいの距離ですか？
   (　　　　　　　　　　　　　　) is it your house from the JR station?

3. コピーを何枚印刷しましょうか？
   (　　　　　　　　　　　　　　) copies should I print?

4. 地下鉄職員の値下げはいくらですか？
   (　　　　　　　　　　　　　　) is the subway's staff discount?

5. 今晩, クリスマスイルミネーションを見に行きましょう。
   (　　　　　　　　　　　　　　) go to see the Christmas lights tonight?

6. 彼女をデートに誘ったら？
   (　　　　　　　　　　　　　　) ask her out on a date?

疑問詞で始まる疑問文は, いつも
「何かを尋ねる文」とは限らない！

3 1 ～ 5 の疑問文と対応する適切な応答文を後半 a ～ e から選び線でつなぎましょう。

1. Are you going to work part time? ・ ・ a Anything. What's up?

2. Why don't you take a deep breath? ・ ・ b If you spend more than 1,000 yen, they will.

3. Can I ask something? ・ ・ c That's a good idea!

4. Do you know the best way to go? ・ ・ d You should check Google Maps.

5. Will they deliver the food? ・ ・ e I'm free this afternoon.

▶▶ 1 ～ 5 で作った英文を日本語に直しましょう。

1. _____

2. _____

3. _____

4. _____

5. _____

4 (A)～(D) の 4 つの短い音声を聴き，写真の内容を最も適切に表現しているものを 1 つ選びましょう。

1 (A) (B) (C) (D)　　　**2** (A) (B) (C) (D)

誤肢（イジワル選択肢）に気をつけ，
音の違いをしっかり聴き取ろう！

★ 81

5A (A)〜(C) の選択肢を日本語に直し，いろいろな種類の疑問文に最も適切に対応しているものに〇をつけましょう。

さあ，この形式に少し慣れてきたかな？
次の問題で力試し！

1. A: Why don't we take a taxi to the station?
   B: (A) We don't need to take a train.

      _____

      (B) We might be caught in a traffic jam.

      _____

      (C) It might not be easy to walk there.

      _____

2. A: Why don't you take a day off?
   B: (A) My pleasure.

      _____

      (B) Give me a hand.

      _____

      (C) That's something I need.

      _____

3. A: Are you staying in Hawaii one more week or moving to another place?
   B: (A) Sure, I can't wait.

      _____

      (B) Yes. I've booked a flight already.

      _____

      (C) Text me when you move there.

      _____

4. **A:** Would you rather go on a picnic or go for a drive?

   B: (A) Either is OK.

   _____

   (B) I'd rather relax.

   _____

   (C) It must be enjoyable.

   _____

5. **A:** Meg is coming to the party tonight, isn't she?

   B: (A) I think she was very busy.

   _____

   (B) I hope she is.

   _____

   (C) No, she hasn't appeared yet.

   _____

6. **A:** I think the fax machine is out of order.

   B: (A) No, there're some problems.

   _____

   (B) I'll ask someone to check it.

   _____

   (C) Yes, why not?

   _____

5B 次に読まれる会話文を聴いてその質問に対する応答として最も適切と思われるものを，(A)〜(C) の 3 つの選択肢の中から 1 つ選びましょう。

1. (A) (B) (C)   4. (A) (B) (C)

今度は同じ問題を聞き取って答えてみよう！

2. (A) (B) (C)   5. (A) (B) (C)

3. (A) (B) (C)   6. (A) (B) (C)

6 図表を読み会話文を聞いて，その質問に対する応答として最も適切と思われるものを，(A)〜(D) の 4 つの選択肢の中から 1 つ選びましょう。

だんだん TOEIC のリアル問題スタイルに近づいてきたよ！

Movie Showtimes	Theater opens 30 minutes before first showing.		
Admission Prices	(All weekend showings, please add $2.)		
	[Adult] Regular Showing—$6.50		3D Showing—$8.50
	[Child] Regular Showing—$3.75		3D Showing—$5.75
Friday, March 8	Captain Marvel (*PG12)	17:30	*PG: Parental Guidance
	3D What Men Want (*R15+)	21:00	*R: Restricted
Saturday, March 9	Captain Marvel (PG12)	13:30	
	Captain Marvel (PG12)	17:00	
Sunday, March 10	Captain Marvel (PG12)	13:00	
	Captain Marvel (PG12)	17:00	
	Wonder Park (PG12)	20:30	
Monday, March 11			
Tuesday, March 12			
Wednesday, March 13			
Thursday, March 14	Closed		

1. How much will Toshi pay for three tickets in total?

登場人物は何人かな？

    (A) $16.75   (B) $19.75
    (C) $21.75   (D) $22.75

2. What time does "Captain Marvel" start on that day?

    (A) At 5:30 p.m.   (B) At 5:00 p.m.
    (C) At 1:30 p.m.   (D) At 4:00 p.m.

3. Why is Toshi getting upset?

    (A) Because he was 30 minutes late to meet his friend.
    (B) Because he was worried about Jeff's mood.
    (C) Because he couldn't convey what he wanted to say.
    (D) Because he was surprised to see so many people at the theater.

日本語の主語を
そのまま英語の主語にしてもいいの？

Q 日本語に対応する英語表現として自然な英語は a，b のどちらでしょう？（　　）に○を書き入れましょう。（20 秒）

1.	シャワーを浴びると目が覚める。 （　）**a.** Taking a shower helps me wake up. （　）**b.** I wake up by taking a shower.
2.	開店は何時ですか？ （　）**a.** What time is the opening of the shop? （　）**b.** What time do you open?
3.	趣味は何ですか？ （　）**a.** What is your hobby? （　）**b.** What do you like to do in your free time?
4.	あなたはなぜ日本に来たのですか？ （　）**a.** Why did you come to Japan? （　）**b.** What brought you to Japan?

上の正解からわかったことは何ですか？自由に書いてみましょう。

Target　（　　　　　　　　　　　　　　　　　　　　　　　　　　　　　　　　　　）

1 次の会話文の中に自然でない英語の表現が 1 つあり，その表現を含む部分に下線を引いています。（　　）に適切な英単語を書き入れ，より自然な表現を完成させましょう。

1. Salesperson:　Hello. May I help you?　いらっしゃいませ。

　　　Takuya:　<u>Does this shop sell rice-flour bread?</u>　このお店，米粉パンありますか？

　　　　　　　（　　　　　　　）（　　　　　　　）（　　　　　　　） rice-flour bread?

2.　　　Bob:　I'm very thirsty. Let's drink something cold!
　　　　　　　とても喉が渇いたね。何か冷たいもの飲みましょう！

　　Mariko:　Oh no! <u>Oolong tea is sold out in the vending machine.</u>
　　　　　　　あら〜！自販のウーロン茶が売り切れだわ。

　　　　　The (　　　　　　　)(　　　　　　　) is sold out of oolong tea.

3.　Cathy:　Nice to meet you, I'm Cathy Baker. Please call me Cathy.
　　　　　　初めまして，キャシー・ベイカーです。キャシーと呼んでください。

　　Takako:　Oh, Cathy. It's nice to meet you. So <u>what is your job?</u>
　　　　　　おお，キャシー，初めまして。お仕事は何ですか？

　　　　　　what (　　　　　　)(　　　　　　) do for a living?

4.　Carol:　I'm Carol. I was born in Canada and was raised in New Zealand.
　　　　　　キャロルです。カナダで生まれニュージーランドで育ちました。

　　Shinji:　I'm Shinji Ogawa. I'm a university student, and <u>my family is five people.</u>
　　　　　　小川慎二です。大学生です。私の家族は5人です。

　　　　　　(　　　　　　)(　　　　　　) five people in my family.

5.　Meg:　I'm very busy because the fall term started last week.
　　　　　　秋学期が先週から始まったから，勉強が忙しいわ。

　　Akiko:　You need to relax a bit. <u>What's your hobby?</u>
　　　　　　じゃ，気晴らしが必要ね。趣味は何？

　　　　　　(　　　　　　)(　　　　　　)(　　　　　　) usually do in your
　　free time?

2　語群から適切な語句を選び（　　）に書き入れ，日本文に合う英文を完成させましょう。
ただし文頭にくる語も小文字で示してあります。

---

convenient for / do you have / there are / the shop was / what does

1.　あなたは火曜と金曜と，どちらのご都合がよいですか？
　　Which is more (　　　　　　　　　　) you, Tuesday or Friday?

2.　両親と姉，私の4人家族です。
　　(　　　　　　　　　　) four people in my family, my parents, my elder
　　sister and me.

3.　失礼ですが，お父さんのお仕事は何ですか？
　　If you don't mind me asking, but (　　　　　　　　　　) your father do?

4.　このお店に有機栽培のお茶はありますか？
　　(　　　　　　　　　　) organic tea?

5.　その店は冬物衣類を売りつくした。
　　(　　　　　　　　　　) sold out of winter clothes.

3 日本語に対応する英語表現として自然な英語は a，b のどちらでしょう？（　　）に○を書き入れましょう。

1. コンビニでアルバイトをしています。
   - （　　）**a.** My part-time job is working at a convenience store.
   - （　　）**b.** I have a part-time job at a convenience store.

2. （注文は）チキンカレーとトマトサラダにします。
   - （　　）**a.** My order is chicken curry and tomato salad.
   - （　　）**b.** I'll have chicken curry and tomato salad.

3. 私の趣味は犬を散歩に連れて行くことです。
   - （　　）**a.** My hobby is taking my dog for a walk.
   - （　　）**b.** I like to take my dog for a walk.

4. 今年は雨がたくさん降りました。
   - （　　）**a.** We had a lot of rain this year.
   - （　　）**b.** This year has a lot of rain.

5. 日本では，子供が減っている。
   - （　　）**a.** Children in Japan are *decreasing.   *decrease: 減少する
   - （　　）**b.** The number of children in Japan is decreasing.

6. この店では，9月にバーゲンがある。
   - （　　）**a.** This store has a sale in September.
   - （　　）**b.** A sale is in September at this shop.

7. この歌を聴くと，昔を思い出します。
   - （　　）**a.** I get nostalgic when I hear this song.
   - （　　）**b.** This song reminds me of my good old days.

4 1 ～ 6 の疑問文と対応する適切な応答文を後半 a ～ f から選び線でつなぎましょう。

1. The number of young people in Japan   •

2. (To a convenience store clerk) Do you have   •

3. What does your brother   •

4. We had very little   •

5. I like to   •

6. We are a family   •

•   **a**   do for a living?

•   **b**   snow last winter.

•   **c**   fruit sandwiches?

•   **d**   sleep on my bed.

•   **e**   of five.

•   **f**   is decreasing.

▶▶ 1 ～ 6 で作った英文を日本語に直しましょう。

1. _____

2. _____

3. _____

4. _____

5. _____

6. _____

5 (A)～(D) の 4 つの短い音声を聴き，写真の内容を最も適切に表現しているものを 1 つ選びましょう。 (58, 59)

1 (A)　(B)　(C)　(D)

2 (A)　(B)　(C)　(D)

6A 広告文を読み，対応する日本語の（　　　）に適切な表現を書き入れましょう。

SUNNY'S YEAR-END SALE
All our towels feel amazing to the touch!

On the week beginning Dec. 21, our shop will have a special sale on towels.
If you buy more than five towels and the total costs over 35 dollars, you can get another towel of your choice and a small present for free.

Goods: All kinds of towels, mats, curtains, cushions, and other lovely goods
Colors: 48 colors!!
Free delivery: Only for this special week
Free wrapping: Only for this special week

No debit cards. No checks. Cash and credit cards only.

Sunny's: 18th Street, Ottawa
TEL: 0123-456-789

サニーズ ¹（　　　　　　　　　　）セール

ここのタオルは ²（　　　　　　　　　　　　　　）

³（　　　　　　　　　　　　）タオルの特別セールを実施します。

⁴（　　　　　　　　　　　　　　），お買い上げ価格が 35 ドルを超えますと，お好きなタオルもう一枚とささやかなプレゼントを進呈致します。

商品：⁵（　　　　　　　　），マット，⁶（　　　　　），クッション，
　　　その他かわいい小物

色：48 色！！

⁷（　　　　　）：セール期間のみ

無料包装：セール期間のみ

デビッドカード，小切手は使用不可。⁸（　　　　　　　　　　　　）のみ

サニーズ：オタワ，18 通り

電話番号：0123-456-789

6B 次に読まれる英文を聴いてその質問に対する応答として最も適切と思われるものを，(A)〜(D) の４つの選択肢の中から１つ選びましょう。

1. What do they have at the shop?
   (A) Various fancy goods
   (B) Towels only
   (C) Bed clothes
   (D) Fabric products

2. What kind of payment do they accept at the shop?
   (A) Cash only
   (B) Credit cards and cash only
   (C) Debit cards only
   (D) Credit cards only

3. On the special week, what do they give if customers spend more than 35 dollars on towels?
   (A) They can get a fee for delivery.
   (B) They can get a discount on wrapping.
   (C) They can get a small gift from the shop.
   (D) They can get one more towel and a small present.

 ~ Take a Break ~

英語の主語を何にする？

日本文を英文に翻訳する際，重要なポイントに「英文の主語を何にする？」があります。なぜなら，日本語は主語を省略する傾向にある言語ですが，英語は基本的に主語が必要だからです。

テキストでは，学習者の間違えやすい日本語表現を扱いましたが，他にもいろいろあります。その例として，
「東京は大阪より暑かった。」
　✕ Tokyo was hotter than Osaka.　　○ It was hotter in Tokyo than in Osaka.
「私の夢はまだ決まっていません。」
　✕ My dream hasn't decided yet.　　○ I haven't decided what I want to do in the future.

このように，字面で直訳するのではなく「いったい何を言おうとしているのか？」日本語を噛み砕いて，英語に変える必要があるということですね。

TOEIC 試験対策問題に挑戦！

1 (A)〜(D) の 4 つの短い音声を聴き，写真の内容を最も適切に表現しているものを 1 つ選びましょう。

（61-63）

1 (A) (B) (C) (D)

3 (A) (B) (C) (D)

2 (A) (B) (C) (D)

2 次の会話文の応答文として最も適切と思われるものを，(A) 〜 (C) の 3 つの選択肢の中から 1 つ選びましょう。

64

1. (A) (B) (C)

2. (A) (B) (C)

3. (A) (B) (C)

4. (A) (B) (C)

5. (A) (B) (C)

6. (A) (B) (C)

7. (A) (B) (C)

8. (A) (B) (C)

9. (A) (B) (C)

10. (A) (B) (C)

3 次に読まれる 2 人または 3 人の会話を聴いて，その質問に対する応答として最も適切と思われるものを，(A) ～ (D) の 4 つの選択肢の中から 1 つ選びましょう。 (65, 66)

1 1.   What are the speakers talking about?

(A) Tomorrow's meeting

(B) The PC failure

(C) The handouts for a meeting

(D) The conference room

2.   What will the woman do next?

(A) Repair a computer

(B) Take a break

(C) Prepare the handouts

(D) See a technician

3.   Where do the speakers probably work?

(A) At an electricity shop

(B) At a coffee shop

(C) At a flower shop

(D) At an office

2 1.   What country are the speakers mainly talking about?

(A) U.K.

(B) Canada

(C) France

(D) U.S.A.

2.   What information does the man give to the woman?

(A) His friend in London

(B) The good season in L.A.

(C) The Christmas season in London

(D) The guest house in L.A.

3.   Why will the woman go to L.A. this winter?

(A) She has a guest house.

(B) She can buy a place in L.A.

(C) She loves the summer months.

(D) She can stay at a guest house.

4 次に読まれるアナウンスと写真に関する問題です。アナウンスを聞き写真を見て，最も適切な答えと思われるものを，(A) 〜 (D) の 4 つの選択肢の中から 1 つ選びましょう。 67

ABC Grocery Store Weekend Discount

Featured Product: Natural spring water (500ml) from Japan

Get a coupon and save!

ABC Grocery Store Membership Card

Card Number: H975312

Valid: March 7, 2019–March 6, 2020

Present this card at the service counter each time you visit.

ABC Grocery Store for an additional 30% off all purchases.

This card may not be shared with other individuals.

If this card is lost, please call 123-456-789.

---

1. Where most likely is this announcement being made?
   (A) At a department store
   (B) At a grocery store
   (C) At a bank
   (D) At a drug store

2. What is indicated about the bottled water?
   (A) It's a new item.
   (B) It's a high-quality product.
   (C) It's Japanese natural spring water.
   (D) It's a popular product.

3. What are shoppers recommended to do?
   (A) To save a little time
   (B) To give a helping hand
   (C) To get more money
   (D) To become a member

5 次の英文の空欄に該当する適切な語（句）を (A) 〜 (D) から選びましょう。

1. The room will be unavailable ------- May 5 while renovations are carried out.
   (A) by   (B) until   (C) on   (D) in

2. Ms. Ishii has detailed knowledge of teaching, ------- worked in the school for over 30 years.
   (A) has   (B) have   (C) having   (D) had

3. During the meeting, Ms. Smith ------- standing at the back of the room.
   (A) remained   (B) waited   (C) sitted   (D) remembered

4. Mr. Iwai won't return from his business trip, so I will have to meet with ------- assistant instead.
   (A) he   (B) himself   (C) him   (D) his

5. Any problems with the computer system should ------- to the supervisor.
   (A) report   (B) have reported   (C) be reported   (D) has been reported

6. The total cost of the project was more than double the initial -------.
   (A) estimate   (B) predicted   (C) expectation   (D) eternity

7. ------- strong sales in its food division, CBA Market finished the year in red.
   (A) Because   (B) Because of   (C) Owing to   (D) Despite

6 次の英文を読んで，その質問に対する応答として最も適切と思われるものを (A) 〜 (D) の４つの選択肢の中から１つ選びましょう。

出典：https://www.statista.com/chart/16269/annual-average-earnings-of-women-and-men-in-three-time-periods/

The annual average income figures for men and women in the U.S. have recently been released. The U.S. is a leading economic superpower, but the chart shows that there is a surprising gap in income between men and women. Women's income is almost double what it was in the period between 1968 and 1982. In the period from 2001 to 2015, however, it was only about 58% that of men.

There are some reasons to explain these results. One reason is that women are more likely to take off work for family and child care than men. Another is that, surprisingly, the U.S. is the only country in the G20 in which *paid maternity leave is not *guaranteed.

*paid maternity leave: 有給育児休暇   *guarantee: 保障する

1. Why is the U.S. labor market still a man's world?
    (A) Women's working ability is very low.
    (B) There is a guarantee that women can take paid maternity leave.
    (C) Women's annual income is lower than that of men.
    (D) Women have to take time for improving themselves.

2. Which is NOT true according to this chart?
    (A) The annual income of men is almost the same throughout the period.
    (B) The income of women in the period from 1968 to 1982 is almost half of the average income in the period from 2001 to 2015.
    (C) Finally, women's income has reached that of men.
    (D) The annual income of women has increased surprisingly.

3. What's most likely to be the main purpose of this research?
    (A) To show the U.S. market is already a woman's world
    (B) To show the inequality between men and women in the labor market
    (C) To show more men helping women's house work than before
    (D) To show there are more women CEOs than men in the U.S.

~ *Take a Break* ~

"Genius is 1% inspiration and 99% perspiration" by Thomas Edison

天才あっても目標達成には努力が必要ですね！

TOEIC で高得点を目指すためには「英文速読力」が欠かせません。多くの受験者が「わかっていたのに，時間が足りなかった……」という悔しい思いをしています。資格試験では，解けるだけでは駄目。本番でいかに早く正解を出せるか，わからない問題は「迷わず捨てる！」勇気が高得点を手に入れるカギとなります。例えば Part 5 では，30 問を 12 分で解答せねばなりません。しかしこれを聞いて，自信を無くしがっかりしてしまうことはありません。日本語と同じように，内容を理解しながらスピードを持って英文を読む能力は，日頃の訓練により必ず身につきます。毎日 10 分から，トレーニングを始めましょう！！かなりの英文読解スピードアップが期待できます。

Time to Start **Learn from Your Errors!** [B-897]
より自然な英語習得のための英語演習

1　刷	2020 年 4 月 1 日	
3　刷	2023 年 3 月 31 日	

著　者	樋口　千春	Chiharu Higuchi
	村田　倫子	Noriko Murata

発行者　南雲　一範　Kazunori Nagumo
発行所　株式会社　南雲堂
　　　　〒162-0801　東京都新宿区山吹町361
　　　　NAN'UN-DO Co., Ltd.
　　　　361 Yamabuki-cho, Shinjuku-ku, Tokyo 162-0801, Japan
　　　　振替口座：00160-0-46863
　　　　TEL: 03-3268-2311（営業部：学校関係）
　　　　　　　03-3268-2384（営業部：書店関係）
　　　　　　　03-3268-2387（編集部）
　　　　FAX: 03-3269-2486

編集者　伊藤　宏実

組　版　H. I

装　丁　Nスタジオ

検　印　省略

コード　ISBN 978-4-523-17897-2　C0082

Printed in Japan

E-mail　nanundo@post.email.ne.jp
URL　　https://www.nanun-do.co.jp/